Who's *Loving* You Now

Dandreka Griggs

DEDICATION

This book is dedicated to my Grandparents, Emma and Eddie B Brooks.

I would also like to dedicate it to my kids and grandkids.

And, to my dad, my best friend, Danny Brooks, and my mom, Sharon Brooks.

And to my cousin, who's like a sister to me, Yolanda ''Opal'' Reed.

To my cousin, Ronnie "Toile," and his wife, Tasha Johnson.

And to all my sisters, brothers, the rest of my family, and to my 85 Family.

ACKNOWLEDGEMENTS

First, I would like to give thanks to an awesome GOD, my creator, for giving me a sound mind and the wisdom to overcome every obstacle that stood before me.

Thank you to my kids for being the push that I have always needed!

And I would like to give thanks to a great friend, Erica Scott, for being there for any and everything I need.

I would like to give thanks to Miya for all her kind words, and a very special thanks to Uncle Rob and my Aunt Debra Brooks for filling in and being what my grandparents were to me. I love you guys so much!

I want to give great love and thanks to my granddaughter, London and grandson, Tavorius Jr. for giving me one of the greatest smiles a grandfather could have.

POEM

To Precious:

The sun to my clouds

The wind to my breath

As I look into your eyes, I can see the steps of forever and never-ending love.

As the nights grew long, and the stars played a sweet love song,

Our hearts grabbed the rhythm of the waterfalls that fell below our feet.

We stood in the midst of passion inside the shadows of thoughts that linger and float

In my mind of hope and prayers that one day I could kiss and hold you once again.

Like thorns to my finger, my heart is aching thinking about the love we once had.

My dreams came to an end and I woke up in tears, pillow wet, and the clouds hung low.

I laid and wandered, ***"WHO'S LOVING YOU NOW?"***

Chapter One

One beautiful Saturday in March 2005, I met who would become the sparkle of my eye and the light to my heart. I was lying awake in bed and noticed my phone was dying. I jumped up and ran to the shower to get ready to go by Beeper Express. I needed to purchase a charger before I lost my best friend due to having no power all night. While I was in Beeper Express talking and laughing with the store owner, in walked a living angel. I immediately froze in my tracks. Her smile was so radiant, and just like Kane from Menace to Society, I had to push up on her. I looked at her smile and said, "Hello, beautiful angel. How are you?"

Still smiling, she said, "I'm great and yourself?"

I told her, "Seeing you made my day heavenly."

Her smile grew, and my confidence grew along with it. I told her my name and proceeded to ask for hers, and she so softly said, "Precious."

"Hello, Monta. It's nice to meet you."

"It's also nice to meet you, Precious. So, ma'am, are you taken?"

"No, are you?" she asked.

I was married, but on the brink of a divorce, so I said, "No." I then asked for her phone number. We exchanged numbers and went our separate ways. For days, I looked at that number thinking, *Should I wait a week to call her or should I just call now?* Hour after hour, I racked my brain over what I should do. I decided to text her and ask her how she was doing. Right away, she texted me back.

Precious: It took you long enough!

With a big smile on my face, I felt a huge relief. Throughout the day, we chatted and enjoyed each other's conversation. Weeks passed, and we became closer and closer until one day I was at home, and she called my phone while I was in the shower. My wife, Shevonne, answered the phone. I could hear yelling and screaming, bad word after bad word, and I knew somebody was in trouble. A few seconds later, there was a loud BOOOM, BOOOM, BOOOM at the door.

"Hold on," I yelled out.

"No, motherfucker! Open this damn door, now!" Shevonne screamed.

I was in the shower, but I yelled out, "I'm on the toilet, Shevonne! You know you don't want to smell this toxic!"

There was more loud pounding on the door before she stopped and said, "I will see you when you come out."

I finished my shower and dried off slowly. I was trying to figure out why she was so pissed. As I was walking out the door, I ran right into her standing there, holding my phone.

"So, Monta, who is Precious?" she asked.

Caught by surprise, I replied, "Who?"

"Oh, motherfucker, you know who. I read the damn messages. Oh, you know who!"

I stuck out my chest with anger and replied, "Give me my damn phone. I don't go through your shit. And aren't we getting a divorce? Why does it matter anyway?"

I snatched my phone and put on my clothes and shoes. I headed to my brother's house while trying to call Precious as I drove, but she didn't answer. I texted her, and still got no reply.

Later that night, I got a text from Precious, saying, *Please don't text or call my phone anymore!*

I deleted her number, and months went by with no contact with Precious. I met other women, but none of them brought me the smile that Precious took from me when she kicked me to the curb. I decided to let it all go and move on as I called up my boys and told them, "Let's burn the streets up on these bikes."

It was nice and sunny on this warm day in June. I washed up the Busa, cleaned the chrome, and we cruised the streets of Alabama. Just when we were heading back to Georgia, I saw a beautiful angel and asked her to pull into the car wash. She turned in, as my guys and I turned the bikes around. As I approached the car, that smile caught my eye. It was like this was our first time meeting all over again. I froze, but she was comfortable.

"Can you pull me?" Precious asked.

"I would love to," I said.

She gave me her number, and later that day, she called and said that she was ready for her ride. I told her to come to West Point, and thirty minutes later, she and her friend pulled up. I was standing there with the helmets in my hand. Precious told her friend to ride first because she was scared. I took her friend around the block and came back. I assured her friend that I would take good care of Precious. I put the helmet on her, she got on, and we took off.

To get more time with the angel, I went a longer route. I allowed her to feel the embrace of a man, and to show her that I was in control, I grabbed her hand and pulled her closer. As I twisted the throttle of the 1536 horses, the wind blew through our helmets. We smelled the sweetness of the flowers on the countryside on that beautiful day. I could feel her relaxing. It felt like our souls had combined at that moment. Knowing her friend was left alone, I hurried to get her back. Precious looked at me and said, "I want to do that again."

"Just call me, and I will take you for a ride anytime," I told her.

"Oh, okay. That sounds like a plan," she said with a smile. Then, she looked at me with those dreamy eyes and said, "Thanks again, Monta."

My heart fluttered from the sound of my name coming off of her lips. I got back on my bike and said, "You're welcome, beautiful."

Every day and every night, we became closer. She would come over to my cousin's house, and we would spend time together. As bad as I wanted to give her that Monta attention, I took my time and made her fall for me by spending time with her and making her feel special. In the process, I fell for her. This was all until one day when Precious and her friend came over, and my homeboy was feeling her friend. I pulled her to the side and told her, "Hook your girl up with my boy. I think he's feeling her."

To my surprise, she said, "I think she's feeling him also."

We set a date for later that night, and we all met up. My homie took her friend to his house, and me and Precious chilled at my cousin's pad. We talked for a while with my cousin and her friends until they started smoking weed. Neither one of us smoked, so we went into the bedroom. She sat on the bed, and I joined her. By the time the door closed, in my head, I was saying, *it's time*, but I wanted to take it slow. I leaned over and gave her a kiss. She gave me that famous smile and said, "Your lips are so soft."

Smiling, I said, "Chapstick every day." I locked lips with her again. I could feel her body shiver. She relaxed as I climbed onto the bed. I started kissing her gently as I felt her melt away under me. I kissed down to her neck slowly while trying not to give her the impression that I wanted to take advantage of her. As I went down further, I introduced my soft lips to her right nipple. I knew that was a sensitive spot from the trembling of her body and the way that she bit her lips and caressed my ears.

I traveled down her sexy body, sliding her pants off. She looked at me with a plea in her eyes that said, *"Don't hurt me."*

I looked into her eyes and said, "I'll be as gentle as the day when we were riding the bike."

She smiled and relaxed. I kissed her while slowly pulling her panties off. Our lips connected in a soft and gentle dance as I lifted her legs. I began to make a song with her sweet notes of moans. I lifted her off the bed like we were replaying Fifty Shades of Grey, but better. I put her on my shoulders and slid her pussy down on my tongue. I was sucking on her clit as she came over and over again. I gave her pleasure women die trying to find, all while being gentle with every touch and stroke of my tongue.

"What are you doing to me? Why is my pussy feeling like this? Why won't my legs stop shaking?" she asked with sweet, sexy moans.

She steadily screamed, "Please, don't stop," as she had about seven orgasms. I laid her down and let her taste the sweetness that I had tasted. As I slid inside of her, I could feel her body tense up. She buried her nails in my back.

"Go slow. You're too big," she pleaded.

I whispered softly in her ear, telling her, "That's all I know."

Keith Sweat played in the background as I moved with strong thrusts in and out. I watched her bite her lips as she wrapped her arms around me while pulling me closer.

"Baby, I feel my soul leaving my body," she said, looking into my eyes.

"Baby, you just felt what real lovemaking is," I told her as she held me tighter and begged me to keep going.

"This is where I want to be forever," she moaned out.

I did my famous 'make her gasp' move. I pulled up, yet not all the way out, and then did a swimmer's dive. Tank played on the radio as I rolled my hips. She took a deep breath and let go.

"Damn, I love you. Do that again," she begged.

I was caught up in the song, as I kept stroking. I flipped her over and gave her that 'I got your back' deep stroke.

She looked back and said, "I'm about to cum!"

I held her close and let her feel my arms around her as she creamed all over me. She pulled me close for one last kiss. We were so into our moment that we didn't even hear her phone ringing.

When we were cleaning up, she looked at me with a shocked expression. "Thirteen missed calls, baby," she said. At that moment, I knew we had gone to that special place that only good lovemaking could take you.

We were headed out the door when she looked at me and said, "Baby, that felt so good."

I licked my lips. "That was so sweet!" I told her. We both laughed as we got into my truck. I drove her back to meet her friend. She jumped out of the truck and got into the car.

"Make sure that you call me when you get home to let me know that you made it safely," I told her.

That night, I couldn't sleep. The scene kept playing back in my mind over and over again. I had to get up and go to work the next morning, so I closed my eyes to try to rest. Less than three hours later, I was awakened by my alarm. I still had the biggest grape Kool-Aid smile.

All day long, all that I could think about was Precious. Her eyes, her lips, her scent, everything about her. That day at work, I had the longest eight hours on the clock. Finally, my phone vibrated with sweet kiss emojis and a *Hey baby!* text message from Precious.

I replied back: *Hey, beautiful. All day long, I couldn't stop thinking of you.*

Precious: I know. I couldn't sleep! I felt your presence and thought about you all day. Can we do it again when I get off of work tonight?

With a big smile, I replied: *Yes, baby. We can do it every day, all day if you like.*

She sent the laughing emoji and replied: *I would love that, but we can't.*

Later that night when she got off, she called me. I told her to stop by my brother's house because that's where I was. She pulled up and said, "Baby, let's get in your truck. I can't wait."

We got in the truck and climbed in the back. I slid my hand in her pants, and her pussy was soaked. She smiled.

"Now, you feel how bad I want you, Monta!" she said. I smiled and slid my finger into her pussy. She pulled my shirt up as if she wanted to rip it off me. By that time, the Brooks boys pulled up wanting to race. I kissed Precious one last time and jumped out of the truck. She got out and started dying laughing at Peter and his loud mouth. We set the race up for the next night because their rider didn't show up.

I couldn't wait for Precious and me to get some privacy. The next day, we all gathered at my brother's house. Precious called and asked had we raced yet because she wanted to see it.

"No, we haven't raced yet, baby. Come on over," I told her. By the time she got there, we had relocated to my sister's house. We were out there getting up the money for the race. Like always, they were asking for something, so we handicapped the race. I went and got on my homeboy's CBR 1000. The first race I beat him, and he said I didn't. The next race wasn't even close. But with them, there was always an argument. Peter said that he didn't lose the first race, while everyone else said that he did. To hear my baby Precious put her two cents in made me smile.

As the night went on, we all hung out and had fun. The next day, my brother called and asked if I wanted to ride when

I got off. He told me to get my girl because he had a friend that wanted to ride. We all met at my brother's house. I didn't have a back seat, so my homie, DJ, and I swapped bikes. He liked riding the Busa anyway. We had to ride to pick up my brother's friend, so we went out to the country. It felt so nice to have my baby on the back of the bike. We cruised behind everyone enjoying the view. I promised her on her first ride that I would always ride safe with her on the bike with me.

We pulled up to my brother's friends' house and waited for her to come out. As she got on the bike, her breasts came out of her shirt. Either she didn't notice it, or she just didn't care. Precious got her attention and let her know she was flashing the whole gang, so she fixed her clothes. We took off riding through West Point, Lanett, and Valley. The gang wanted to stop by a club to have some drinks. Some of us didn't drink, and a few people weren't old enough to get in, so we rolled on. We were cruising through Valley, and then we hit the interstate.

I was still cruising when Precious leaned up close to my ear and said, "Go fast, baby!" And oh, boy, what did she say that for?

I grabbed her hand, pulled her to me, and twisted the throttle. We reached one-forty-five in no time. As it climbed to one seventy, she laid her head on me and squeezed tight. I felt the relaxation of her body. She knew that she was safe and safe she was. As we got off the exit, she leaned up close to my ear and said, "I love it when you do that."

"Do what, baby?" I asked.

"Pull me close to you like that. It makes me feel so safe."

I had the biggest smile that helmet had ever seen. Even though I wanted to taste her that night, I took her home and gave her a goodnight kiss.

As I woke up the next day, my brother called to tell me to get ready. He said, "We're loading up and going to the track."

I got ready and headed to my brother's house. As we were strapping the bikes down, Precious called and asked what I was doing. I told her we were getting ready to go to the track, and she asked if she and her friend could go.

"Come on, baby. You know you can go," I told her. "We will be leaving here shortly."

"Okay, baby. We are on our way."

"Okay, see you when you get here," I said. Three minutes later, she turned in slow as if she was in a photoshoot with that sweet smile. I could watch that smile all day long, and it would make me happy.

We got into the truck and double-checked everything. Low and behold, my cousins pulled up. The get-right crew was Opal (who we called Op) and Tara (who we called T). They ran up, screaming that they wanted to go. Big Truck, my brother, said jokingly, "We'll strap y'all asses on the trailer with the bikes."

Oh, boy, what did he say that for? Already high and tipsy, the get-right crew jumped on the hood of the truck, screaming, "Let's go! Shit, we ready." We laughed our asses off while making room for them.

It was beautiful and sunny out but not too hot, which made for great racing weather. As we pulled into the gates, we saw the crowd before we topped the hill. The girls were in shock because it was their first time going, and we were the hometown favorites. My bike, Taz, was on the back looking mean, and the Roadrunner was looking mean too. With four beautiful women by our sides, we were unstoppable that day. Just like every other weekend that we pulled up to the track.

As we started down the hill, my brother spotted our first victim. We unloaded the bikes and negotiated a race for five hundred dollars. All day long, Taz raised hell. Win after win, it felt good to have my queen next to me and my crew with that strong support. As the night started winding down, I realized I hadn't spent time with my baby. I stepped away and watched some racing with her. I wanted to let her know that, even though I was in my element, she was still the center of my attention.

The announcer said the staging lanes would be closing in ten minutes, and we started loading the bikes. Some local guys called us out on the Roadrunner—gas for gas. We never ran my bike on gas, but we took a gamble anyway. We pulled the bike off the trailer, hooked up the nitrous bottle, and pushed it to the starting line. With the time winding down, they wanted to argue about the pot while trying to out bet us because they really didn't want to race. They called a twenty-five-hundred-dollar pot. As a crew, Truck and I didn't have to say anything. The ladies called it, and we counted out our money. We gave it to the trackman and waited for them to hand over their twenty-five hundred. Low and behold, they only had six hundred. Since they wasted our time, we ran it for six hundred.

We started the bikes, got in the water box, and started the burnout. My nitrous wouldn't come on. Knowing I was a better rider, it didn't matter. I turned on my first bulb and waited for him to turn his on. He pulled in and turned both bulbs on. Right then, I knew the race was won. As I slowly rolled in, the light dropped. I tore out the hole three bikes on him before he even moved. And what would you know? My nitrous hit, and when it did, it hit hard. The bike came off the ground, and I went across the finish line on the back wheel. My competition was nowhere in sight.

I came up the return lane and saw my crew.

"Did you get the money?" I asked.

Before my brother could say anything, Precious said, "We got the money when he turned both his bulbs on. Your brother said he lost when he activated both his bulbs and that you were going to cut his head off. That you did, baby. I'm so proud of you! And I love you. Let's go so I can have the rest of this night with you."

"I would love that," I said. I loaded up, locked down, and went down the road with my baby in the front seat with me. Driving under the night sky was beautiful. She grabbed my hand and put it between her legs. I was so distracted that I drove off the road. Everybody screamed.

"Damn, boy! What are you doing up there?" my brother yelled out.

Laughing, I said, "That damn gator jumped out in front of me." My brother was the only one who knew what I was talking about.

My baby looked at me with those doe eyes that held a bit of wonder in them. "Every time I see you on a bike, that's what it does to me. It makes me so wet," she whispered close to my ear.

"Let me dry it up for you, baby," I whispered close to her ear, and that beautiful smile of hers was brighter than the headlights. It was just something about her that made me melt to the sound of her voice. It was like a Sunday morning with the singing birds. Her eyes glowed like the finest diamond, and her pillow lips hypnotized me at the first touch. She was my perfect mate. To have someone I could enjoy, have fun with, make love to, and have my back no matter what was worth killing for. That was my Precious. Then, I had to get back to reality. I still had a wife at home because our divorce wasn't final.

As we pulled up to my brother's house, I knew our time was limited. I told my brother I was just going to back the trailer in and for him to leave the bikes on the trailer. I would come and unload them tomorrow. He already knew where my mind was, so he gave me the thumbs up. Things didn't work out as I planned; Precious had to take her friend home. I kissed her goodnight and told her that we would make time for each other tomorrow. I floated home with my head all in the clouds. I was still bumping Keith Sweat, and my heart was warm from that kiss. Knowing what I had as a mate and that tomorrow would be beautiful, I regretted going home. However, I made it to the house and took a shower.

I thought I was going to bed, but Shevonne wanted to argue. She was lying in bed on the phone talking to her boyfriend, which was okay with me. She started screaming at me when she hung up with him. I smiled through the entire argument. I was still high off Precious, and nothing Shevonne had to say would bring me down. Finally, she got tired of trying to argue with me and fell asleep.

I couldn't sleep. I was still thinking about my night at the racetrack with Precious. My phone went off with a sweet text, saying, *Baby I can't wait until I'm in your arms tomorrow. I love you. Goodnight!*

That had me like a kid on Christmas, but damn Santa. I wanted Precious.

Chapter Two

The next morning, I woke up to an empty house and no keys. I knew Shevonne had my keys because I always put them in the same place. I called her phone, and it went to voicemail. I must have called two hundred times, and I kept getting her voicemail. Precious called to tell me she would be ready in an hour, and I said, "Okay," knowing I might not be able to make it.

Forty minutes passed, and my calls were still going to Shevonne's voicemail. Remembering I had an extra key in my sock drawer, I grabbed it and jumped in the truck. As I was about to pull off, Shevonne pulled in and blocked my truck. She must have had a sixth sense to know I'd just found my other key. She looked angry because I had that key. She threw the keys in the window and yelled, "You can't get out, motherfucker."

Me, being a smart ass, I drove around the house laughing, but what did I do that for? She jumped in her car to follow me, and even though she didn't know which way I went, she knew where I was going. I called Precious and told her to meet me at my sister's house, and we arrived at the same time. Seeing my queen took all the worries and problems away. I jumped in her car, and she asked me to drive, so we swapped seats.

"Baby, I need my windows tinted. Every time I come over here, somebody is always looking in my car and trying to stop me," Precious was saying as Shevonne passed us. She didn't know what kind of car Precious had, so we were good.

I drove to my other house, the one my cousin and I had together. This was where I went when I needed to clear my head and just relax. I stuck the key in the door and began to turn it. Before I could get the door open, Precious jumped into my arms and squeezed me tight. She started kissing and sucking on my lips, kissing my neck, and everywhere that her mouth could reach. She kicked the door closed and pulled her dress up. As I picked her up, she wrapped her legs around my neck. When I heard the lock click to the locked position, we went up the stairs. I felt her holding on tight, and I knew that she was losing her mind.

In that house, we had fifteen steps. From step one to step ten, she came four times. From step ten to the bed, she came three more times. When I put on Johnny Gill, we were stroking with the motion. The first ten minutes was our introduction. It was as if we were flipping through the tracks trying to find that perfect selection. Then, when we changed positions, the song changed. When Tank hit that note slowly, we tuned in to the baby-making action as she drove her nails into my back. Her tears started flowing, and as the tears flowed, the passion grew greater. When we hit the peak of perfection, she zinged. Her soul locked with my soul, and our hearts beat at the same rhythm. It was so intense that we didn't know it was 3 a.m. We had been there for ten hours and didn't even know it. We laid there talking and laughing. We were making plans and weren't worrying about what tomorrow would bring. I had to be at work in three hours and didn't care.

We got cleaned up, and I took her home. I made it home and didn't even bother to lay down. I just took a shower and headed to work. That day, Precious and I talked all day long. It was something about that night that was different. From that day forward, things weren't going to be the same. That night sent our love and respect to another universe.

"Monta, I want to spend forever with you. If not forever, then right here with you is where my heart stands and will stay," she'd said those words to me, and I smiled, knowing this was what I wanted also.

I got off work knowing that I would soon have my baby in my arms. I hurried home to get dressed so that I could meet up with Precious. My phone rang as I was pulling out the yard. Precious was on the other end. I told her to meet me at the house. When she pulled up, the air was different. Our greeting was different. The kisses were more affectionate. We went upstairs where my cousin and her son were, and that day he fell in love. I told him to sit his little pissy ass down somewhere. Precious laughed and called me pissy.

"No, you and him both are pissy," I teased, and that kind of stuck with us. Every time we saw each other, we used the nickname pissy.

Thursday rolled around. I got off work and needed to see my baby, but she had to work. I went to my brother's and hung out with the guys until she got off. We were chilling, talking about our everyday thing (racing) when the Brooks boys pulled up with a new bike.

The bike was nice and pretty, but was it fast? They went into the garage and worked on the bike, getting it ready. As they turned the last bolt, they called us out.

My brother didn't do much racing, but this particular day the Brooks boys pissed him off, so we went to the backyard immediately. It felt funny with me not riding the bike, but to see Truck on it, I knew this shit was about to go down. When we got to the spot, Truck lined up with Dave, the older Brooks' brother.

I was the flagman, so I lined them up, got the set, and made sure they were ready. When I dropped my hands, my brother tore up out of there. I'd seen him race before, but this time was different. He was racing with an attitude.

When he crossed the line, he was seven or eight bikes ahead. He immediately turned around and lined back up and told the other Brooks brother, Pete, to get his ass on the bike, and he got the same treatment. I could tell he was hot. The Brooks boys had pissed Truck off so bad that he rode Taz better than he ever had before. This time, when he turned around, he didn't even stop. He just kept going.

When we got back to the house, he was sitting in the yard with a cigarette and a Coors Light. That day, he road Taz better than I ever did. Not long after we got back to the house, Precious called and said that she was on her way. Three minutes later, she pulled in and noticed the frustration on Truck's face. She knew there was something wrong. Since he treated her like his little sister, it was easy for her to talk to him. She asked him what was wrong, and the story began.

He told her how the whole situation happened and how the race went down. The excitement on her face was priceless.

After their conversation, we walked to her car and talked about what we wanted for our future. Then, she told me that she really needed her windows tinted. I promised to get them done that weekend. The smile on her face was everything I needed. I needed her, and she wanted me, but we sadly had to exchange our goodnight kisses. She had an early morning, and I had an even earlier morning.

Every time our lips touched, my whole body melted. There was just something about her beautiful soul, sexy eyes, and tender lips, not to mention that pretty face. That combination was hard to beat. Just like a 9mil stroker motor, with the right chassis work, it's consistent. After our fairytale kiss, we said our goodnights.

The next morning, I woke up ready to go to work because I knew the end of the day would bring me greatness. Low and behold, it was just that. Precious called me saying she had to see me. She said her body was calling my name all day long. As bad as I wanted to spend my time enjoying more than our artwork when we got together, my brush wanted to create a masterpiece on her canvas. The way our bodies moved, I could have sworn that I was Vincent van Gogh creating "The Starry Night."

Like always, when we got into the studio, we made nothing but hit records. After our session was over, we relaxed and watched TV for a while. Then, I took her to get something to eat. We went for a long walk and laughed, enjoying each other's company. In the middle of a great conversation, my mechanic called telling me to bring the bike to him tomorrow. I asked my baby if she had to work, and she said no. I told my mechanic that Precious and I would be up there when I got off.

The next day, time slowed down. I had a lot to do. I wanted to get off, load the bike, and head up the road to Atlanta. It seemed like 5 p.m. would never get there. Finally, the clock hit 5:00, and I ran out of the door. My phone rang before I could pick it up to dial Precious' number.

"Hey, baby, what you doing?" I asked.

"Waiting on your pissy ass," Precious said.

"Well, baby. I just got in the truck, but I'm on the way. I will call you when I get out of the shower."

"Okay, baby, and please don't let it take you forever. You know you're slower moving than a woman," she said, teasing me.

"Well, at least you know that I'm clean," I shot back. "But baby, I won't take long, I promise."

I made it to the house, rushed in, and jumped into the shower. When I finished showering, dried off, and put my clothes on feeling fresh and smelling good. I headed out the door and called my baby to tell her that I was finished. It was no surprise that she was waiting for me when I pulled up to my brother's house. The bike was already loaded up, so all that I had to do was hook it up to the trailer and leave. Everything went smooth. I put my guy Keith Sweat in the CD player, and we hit 85 North. That hour and a half was the best ride ever. I was listening to great music and having a great conversation with the greatest woman alive. It was all that a man could ask for.

As we got off on the Cascade exit, I called Harry to meet me at the store. His "I will be there in five minutes" lasted an hour. It was okay because it gave us more time to enjoy each other. We played, laughed, kissed, and then played and laughed some more.

She looked at me and softly and sweetly said, "Monta, I'm so in love with you. I mean, you're not like most guys. You're sweet, gentle, and kind. You show your love by spending time and having passion for others. The way you treat me is unbelievable. I appreciate every bit of your respect and dedication to me and my heart. I wish I could be your wife. I don't think you understand the power you have over me and my mind. The things you do to me are unspeakable. Never heard of! The way you hold me when you are riding the bike. I mean, you can be going almost two hundred miles per hour. Yet, you still make sure I'm safe and comfortable. It's wonderful that, even at a dangerous moment like that, you think of others. I couldn't ask for a better man."

"Thanks, baby! I just be doing my job as your man. I wouldn't have it any other way. You show me the same love and respect. Precious, you have been my breath since the first day I met you, and you are the breath that's in me. If you left, I would be breathless," I told her.

"See, Monta. That's why I love you. You can take words and build a story with them. I have never met nor felt anyone like you. I don't think I will ever find this what we have again."

"I know because I'm the baddest thing since shoestrings. You don't have to tie me. You can just Velcro me together!" I replied.

"That's so lame, Monta. Only old people say shit like that!"

"Yeah, but you love this old person."

"Yes, I do. Now, stop and get me something to eat. I'm hungry!"

"Okay, baby. What do you want?"

"You can stop at Burger King."

"Are you sure? That's not up to queen status."

"Boy, you better stop and get me something to eat."

"Yes, ma'am!"

"You know, baby, I really enjoyed you. I always enjoy you, Monta. I just hate when our night ends."

"Well, it doesn't have to end."

"I know, but we both know it does."

"Precious, I would love for you to be my wife, share your life with me. I have never been so happy in all my years. I can promise you that it will only get better for years to come."

As we got closer to the West Point exit, I could already feel the void of her leaving me. Hopefully, it wouldn't always be this way. I turned into my brother's yard and saw the guys chilling under the tree. In my head, I already knew it was a race cooking up, but my baby was a second away from leaving me.

As I dropped the trailer and parked the truck, a crowd rushed over. Everybody talked at the same time, and the only thing I could hear was, "LaGrange!"

I was still stuck thinking about Precious, who was about to part ways from me for the night. I walked her to the car and kissed her goodnight. Like a kid in the candy store, I stood in the middle of the road like my momma had just told me I wasn't getting any damn candy.

After I had my sensitive moment, I ran over to see what the big fuss was about. We had a race for the next day, and I needed to get home to get some rest. So I made it home, took a shower, and laid it down. As always, I couldn't sleep. Precious was running through my mind, spilling out all through my body, and drowning my heart. I finally closed my eyes, and in no time, my clock was going off.

I jumped out of bed, ready to get this day started. I went to work, hoping this day would go by fast. I needed to call my homie, Telly, so he could tint my baby's windows for me. Before I could get my phone out, it started going off.

"Hey, beautiful!" I said to Precious.

"Hey, baby. You working hard?"

"Not really. Just ready to get off so I can see you."

"I'm ready to see you also, Pissy."

"Umm, no ma'am. That's you, but I love you still."

"Aw, I love you more, Monta."

"Baby, let me call Telly and see if he can do your tint and at what time tomorrow. I will call you back," I hung up the phone with Precious and dialed up Telly.

"What's good, homie?"

"Nothing much."

"Hey, Telly. I need you to tint a car for me tomorrow. Do you think you can handle that for me?"

"Yeah, I can do that, probably around two."

"Okay, well, I will call you around that time."

"Okay, that will work."

I called Precious back and let her know that we were on to get her windows tinted at two the next day. She told me that she had to work. We decided that we could switch cars that night, and she would drive my truck to work.

"What are you doing when you get off later, my love?" Precious asked.

"I was planning to see you."

"Well, let's make that plan work then because you know I need to see you."

"Baby, you will, for the rest of our lives."

"Well, let me go hit this clock. I will see you shortly, beautiful."

"Sounds great to me. Can we ride the bike today?"

"Baby, you know we took the bike to Atlanta."

She said, "Oh, I forgot. See if you can get your brother's bike."

I told her, "I will just call DJ and get his bike."

"Oh, okay. Love you."

"I love you also, my beautiful queen!" I hung up with Precious and called DJ.

"What you doing, homie?"

"Shit. About to head to work," he said.

"Let me use the bike. My baby wants to ride, and my bike's in the shop."

"Okay, you know where it is. I will just leave the key in it," he said.

"Oh, okay," I said and called Precious back to let her know we were on to ride.

"Baby, I will be ready when you are," I told her.

"Well, I'm ready now!" she said, sounding excited.

"Oh, okay then. Pull up."

"Monta, that's why I love you so much. You always cater to my needs. I mean, I can have fun with you. Everything doesn't have to always be serious."

"That's what love's all about. You have to be best friends to have a strong, lasting relationship. You have to enjoy each other's laugh and have fun, not just go through the motions."

"Well, let us start going through these motions with this bike, Monta."

"Oh, shit. I hear you, baby! Let's do the damn thing."

Off we went, turning blocks on this beautiful day. I had the love of my life on the back of the bike. She leaned in and laid her head on my back. At that moment, I felt her take a deep breath and exhale as if she didn't have a care in the world. As we cruised the streets, my mind kept wondering about how our life would be as husband and wife. She was all I ever wanted and needed. We were best friends, and we got along very well. Our time was always spent well when we were together. Sometimes, I wondered if it was too good to be true or if we were just a perfect match.

Precious Griggs does sound good, I thought. I just didn't want to move too fast. Hold on, was I pussy whipped? My thoughts weren't normal for me, but she was different. Her love was genuine. I was thinking of confessing my love to her when we stopped. I was comfortable around her. My heart was attached to the stars with every conversation we had.

I pulled into a parking space, and we walked toward the bench holding hands. I wiped off the bench because I didn't want to share her with anything else. Not even the pine straws. As I looked into her beautiful eyes, my mind and heart had a lot to say. I just couldn't make my lips spell out the words. I took a deep breath, dropped my head, bit my lip, and looked up. I felt my soul push out the words my heart had been creating.

"Precious, I know we have had this talk before. It might just seem like words, but they're words my heart has been sketching in my memory bank for some time now. What we have isn't just a fling or a mistake. We met, lost touch, and met again. For some reason that day, of all the bikes and guys around me, I was the one who turned the page in your book. This isn't some short story that we wrote. I really know in my soul that this book will make history. And even if we do have a hiccup or two every now and again, baby, I promise that you are worth every burp that comes along with it. We have been talking for a few months now, and my heart already knows what it wants. It's you. I got it bad, and I can't help it."

"Well, Monta, I'm in love with you also. Why do you think I make it my priority to see you every day? If I have to work, I make sure I come as soon as I get off."

"Yes, you do, and that's well appreciated," I said.

"Hold on, baby. Somebody is calling me. My butt keeps vibrating." I answered my phone, and it was Yoshi.

"What's up? What's good, Yoshi?"

"I'm finished with your bike," he said.

"Okay. How much do I owe you?"

"It's just nine hundred."

"Okay. I will be up there tomorrow when I get off."

I hung up from Yoshi, turned to Precious, and asked her, "So, baby. Do you want to ride with me tomorrow to get the bike?"

"Yes. You know I do."

"Okay. Well, we better head back because it's getting dark."

We hopped on the bike and started putting our helmets on when I turned around and asked, "Precious, can you promise me forever?"

"Monta, why would I do that and set us up for failure? I want that with you; I just can't make that promise," she said in a soft tone that let me know she was sincere.

"I want it with you also. I will do everything in my power to make that happen, Precious."

As we headed back down the road, I could feel her hand rub my stomach. Her head laid on my back as we both thought about our future. Damn. I didn't want this night to end. We pulled up to my brother's house where her car awaited her, and our goodnight kisses began.

"I love you, Monta."

"I love you, my Precious. Call me when you make it home."

"Okay. I will, baby."

***

The next day rolled around, and work was almost over. My mind was going a hundred miles an hour when my phone went off. It was my baby.

"Hey, Monta!"

"Hey, beautiful!"

"Baby can my friend ride with us to go pick up the bike?" she asked.

"I don't care. As long as my Precious is beside me, I don't care who rides with us," I said. I then headed home to take a shower so that I could get up the road. Everything went smooth as I made it to the house. I showered and then headed to my brother's house to hook up the trailer. As I pulled up, I saw our usual racing crowd, but my mind was on getting up the road. My lady and her friend got there, and we loaded up and took off.

The trip was nice and quick, but we had to wait for Yoshi. Ten minutes later, he pulled up, and we followed him to the house. We were loading the bike up when, out the corner of my eye, I saw Yoshi checking my lady's friend out. He pulled me to the side and proceeded to ask about her. I called Precious and her friend and told them to step out of the truck. They walked over to the trailer where we were standing.

Yoshi yelled, "Monta told me he was bringing a skinny ass girl with him so that I could meet her."

"That's a damn lie because he didn't even know she was coming," Precious said, catching him in his lie. All that we could do was laugh.

Yoshi helped me finish locking the bike down, and we headed down the road. Even though we had a passenger, it was like we were riding alone. Our conversation was like it always was, a lot of laughter and being silly. The trip seemed to go by quickly, no matter how slow I tried to drive. As we came up to our exit, my mind and hers connected with the same thoughts and feelings. Our bodies touched without movement.

We pulled up to my brother's house. They jumped out of the truck, got into her car, and took off. Not even ten minutes later, she returned without her friend. When she looked at me, I already knew what my role was. We got into the cars and headed to the apartment. We went up the stairs kissing like tomorrow would never come. Aggressively, she pulled me into the room. It didn't matter what room as this wasn't our usual room. It was so intense that the heat surrounding our bodies could be felt. Precious snatched her clothes off and put her pussy in my face.

"Do your artwork," she moaned.

I happily started drawing. Every time she came, I could feel the pressure from her hips that were attached to the legs that gripped my head. After several orgasms, I flipped her over. For the first time, I hit it from the back. With every stroke, she screamed, "Go deeper." The deeper I went, the louder she cried. Pounding harder and harder, she got wetter than ever, looking back at me as if she didn't want me to stop.

"Baby, I can feel you in my stomach, but please don't stop," she whined. The pain in her eyes caused me to slow down to steady, slow strokes.

Xscape started playing in my head.

"Take your time and work me slowly."

I got lost within myself again, creating what women die trying to experience. She rolled that ass back, screaming, "Baby, I'm about to cum again."

The greatest magic of that night was to release with her. I hit that famous finishing move of mine, and together we sang the greatest song ever. It was just something about her that drove me crazy. My mind, body, and soul craved her presence.

After we cleaned up and were getting ready to leave, her legs buckled. "Damn, baby, what's wrong?" I asked.

"Shit, you got me weak! I won't be able to walk or wipe after that. You got her all swollen."

"I'm sorry, baby, but you were the cause of all that heat."

Precious reached her hand out to mine and said, "Ha, real funny, Monta. Hold my hands. I can't walk down the stairs without you."

"Really, baby? Do I need to carry you? Get on my back."

"If I get on your back, she will be pressed against your back, and that won't feel good. I will just walk," she whined as she looked at the stairs.

I told her, "Baby, those are a lot of steps to fall down."

"Monta, I'm not going to fall. Just let me hold onto you, and I will be okay."

"Baby, you will be okay regardless because your king is here. Call me when you get home, okay? I love you, pissy."

"I love you more, Monta."

Chapter Three

I woke up the next morning to twenty-five missed calls from my baby and my brother. I got up, showered, and then called my baby first. She wanted to let me know that she wanted to go to the track later. I hung up with her and called my brother. Truck was screaming as soon as he answered the phone.

"Get your ass up, and let's go! I already got the bikes loaded up, so just come on!" he said.

"Okay. Let me call my baby back and let her know we are going now."

I redialed Precious' number. "Hey, baby, are you ready to go now?" I asked when she answered.

"Yes, I been ready."

"Okay, well, come over Truck's house."

"Okay, and baby. My friend wants to go."

"Well, y'all better come on."

"We'll be there in a few minutes."

When I pulled up to my brother's house, he had already hooked up to the trailer and was ready to go. My phone rang, and on the other end, I heard my baby's sad voice.

"What's wrong?" I asked.

She broke my heart by saying that she wouldn't make it because she had to do someone's hair. She said that her friend, Ry, still wanted to go. By that time, Ry turned into the yard, so she, my brother, and I headed to the track. The line was all the way to the road as we turned into the track.

Damn, this motherfucker is packed, I thought. It took us forty-five minutes to get inside. When we did get in, the crowd was yelling, "There go that damn Taz!"

Like always, as we started down the hill, my brother found a victim. We didn't even pull Taz off. We played with my bike until night fell. Then, we brought the monster out. The first race of the night was a big hitter from Atlanta, Mr. Frazier. We got the pot up, and what do you know? Everybody was betting with Mr. Frazier. We did our burnouts, he rolled in the beams and turned on his first bulb. He turned on his second bulb, and I slowly rolled in. As the light dropped, I left first.

When I say Taz was high off that dope that night after being locked down all day, he showed his ass! Across the line we went, first. I had just beat the top dog of drag racing. The king himself. We stopped in the return curve, and he said we had to do that one again. I went back to the staging lane, where my crew met me. My brother checked my eyes and my heart and said, "Boy. You and Taz must be high on that shit tonight the way you tore out of there. The whole starting line said, 'he won't catch him; it's over.'"

I pulled my brother to the side and told him, "Mr. Frazier wants to run it back."

Truck said, "Hell, run it back then! Do you feel it?"

I looked at him and Taz and said, "Push me in the water box."

We started the burnouts. Again, Mr. Frazier pulled in first and turned on his second bulb. Again, I slowly rolled in, and the light dropped off. I tore up out of the hole first. Out of my right ear, I could hear his nitrous kick in. In my mind, I was saying, *You should have saved that.* I started cracking off the line, and Taz shook all the dust off that night. We beat the baddest team that Atlanta had to offer twice that night. I rolled Taz back to the trailer, and the whole track was there waiting on us. My boy, Harry, was the first smile I saw.

"Boy, you hell! You just beat our top shooter twice! I thought you would have had to play catch up, but you cut his head off both times. So, remind me to never race you," Harry said, and all I could do was laugh.

Then, my brother walked up and handed me a beer. "Here, boy. Drink this so you can cool your ass off because you are steaming hot tonight!"

We loaded the bikes up and said goodnight to the homies. We went down the road with a pocket full of money and two badass bikes on the back. The only thing I was missing was my baby. By the time we got to my brother's house, she was already sitting there waiting for us. I backed the truck in the yard, and we sat outside and talked until 3 a.m. I don't think my night could have ended any better. I had the love of my life, my brother, and her friend was chilling with us on this beautiful night. To top it all off, I'd just whipped some ass and made money. What more can a man ask for?

It broke my heart to have to end our time sitting underneath the midnight moon. Tomorrow was Sunday, and I didn't miss church for anyone.

"Baby, you know I love you. I wish that you were lying in my arms at night, but we will get there," I said to Precious. "Please call me so we can go out and spend some of this money tomorrow, okay?"

"I will, baby. I love you!"

"I love you too, beautiful!"

***

It felt as if I'd only been asleep five minutes when my clock started going off like crazy. It was time to get up and get ready for church. I got out of bed and got me and the kids ready to head out the door. Outside, the sun smiled down at me with a shine I had never seen before. Even the sun knew that I was in love. It was that obvious.

The church was packed when we arrived, but the day went by smooth and fast. Finally, I could enjoy my baby and just relax. I returned home, changed my clothes, and called Precious to see if she was ready. I got no answer, so I was worried. That never happened before.

When Precious called me back, I said, "Baby, I thought someone had kidnapped you. I was about to load up and come rescue you."

"Really, Monta? I was in the bathroom."

"So, are we going out, baby? I'm ready."

"Yes, but I have to do something for my mom first!"

"Oh, okay. Just call me when you're done. I will be waiting, baby. I love you, beautiful."

"I love you too, Monta!"

"Well, I guess I will go turn some blocks on the bike," I said.

A few minutes later, I pulled up at my brother's house. The street was packed on both sides, and the bike was on the back of the truck. Somebody was talking shit about their riding skills, so I jumped out the Tahoe ready to mount up. This race wasn't pointed at us this time. They were loaded up headed to LaGrange. For once, we would be watching a race instead of racing in it. For some strange reason, I saw Taz being pulled.

"Cat Daddy, what are we doing with Taz?" I asked.

"We running Terrance on it!"

"Oh, okay, so who's riding it?"

"Boo Boo is going to ride, but he is riding as Slick."

"Oh, so they are going to change riders. Gotcha."

We arrived at the spot and got our money together, but they went back and forth about who was going to win. Finally, they rolled the bike out. We handed the money to the potholder and headed to the road where the race was taking place. They did their burnouts and lineup. As soon as the lights came on, I could hear Taz cutting up, and he left the opposition sitting still. It was an easy three grand. We collected the money, loaded up, and headed back down the road.

As soon as we got off the exit, Precious called asking my whereabouts. We made it back to my brother's house, and my angel was sitting there waiting for me. We planned to go out, but she had other ideas, so we just sat in the car talking. We had a great conversation and laughs. It wasn't what I was expecting, but any time with her was great to me.

As the night went on, she looked at me with a worrisome face. She kissed me so deeply and for so long that I knew this was a passion that I'd never felt before. Being caught up in the moment, I didn't even think to ask her what was on her mind. She looked at me with watery eyes and turned her head away so I couldn't see the pain covering her lovely face.

"Goodnight," Precious softly whispered. "I love you."

"I love you, too, beautiful," I said. Before I could ask her what was on her mind, she kissed me again, squeezing me tightly. Having the bond we had, I could feel her pain flowing through my veins. Every time I tried to pull away to ask her what was wrong, she would squeeze tighter. Instead of trying to figure out the problem, I just did what she wanted and embraced her with love and understanding.

She laid her head on my shoulder and cried like someone had died. I just held her and let her have her peace. Sometimes trying to figure out the problem only creates bigger problems. Knowing the love of my life was in pain made me throw up that king protection around her. As her tears flowed, I wiped them away and kissed her forehead. As her face lit up, she kissed me back, sliding her tongue between my lips, exploring my mouth. She climbed in my lap, playing that slow tone of Johnny Gill, "Take Me I'm Yours."

We went back to the apartment and quickly climbed the steps. I put on my selection of slow grind music on YouTube™. The thunder started rolling, and lightning started flashing on what had been a clear, beautiful night. The first selection came on, and the sweet voice of Johnny began to sing, "Let's get the mood right." I was ten steps ahead of Johnny. I planned to take all her pain away.

We were so caught up in each other that we didn't notice we were lying in bed without a stitch of clothing. Before I could introduce my tongue to her womanhood, she gasped for air as if I had swallowed her clit. That was my plan of action. I just hadn't made it that far yet.

The night went slow. It was like we had frozen time as our bodies played a game of Twister, and so did our minds. The moments were intense. We didn't even notice we were in the room. I had an out of body experience for the first time. It was like I was sitting up watching our bodies make music. It was magnificent to watch my tongue turn flips in and out of her as she bit her lips and arched her back while moaning and clawing my back. She screamed my name in a low and sexy note.

"Baby, slide your dick inside me. Let's paint," she moaned out sexily.

I kissed my way to her nipples, sliding my dick in her slowly, trying not to cause any pain. At the moment, I felt a sharp pain in my shoulder. I looked over to see her teeth locked on me like a pit bull in a dog fight. I eased up just a little, and she slowly let go. Our souls still watched the freak show as Robert Kelly's "Remote Control" came on, and my body went in action. The way that we moved to those lyrics was like something out of a sexual script, but better. It was as if this would be our last time together; it went so well.

She moaned, "Baby, I'm about to cum."

I looked into her eyes and could see the tears rolling down her face, not knowing that I had matching tears. We experienced something only heard about in romantic fairytales. At that moment, we lived it. As we finished, she looked over at me and said, "Baby, I don't know who taught you or where you learned this shit from. But you can bottle this up, sell it, and I promise you that I would buy every bottle."

I assured her, "You don't have to buy something that's already yours."

At 5:30 a.m., we headed back over to my brother's house, so that I could get my truck. I didn't give a damn about the time of morning. I'd just spent some amazing time with the beat of my heart.

She leaned over and kissed me, saying, "I will love you forever, Monta. You have made me a grown woman in every way, and you have given me a new respect for love and loving someone. I knew the first time I saw you in that store that you were special in your own way. But, now, I have experienced that uniqueness you possess, and I know I will never find that again. You are beautiful and sweet. You have respect for yourself and others. That will take you a long way in life. If someone pisses you off, just call me, and I will come running."

"Baby, you have also given me a new respect for the meaning of love and lovemaking." I paused and looked deeply into her eyes. I loved this woman beyond measure, so I hated to have to tell her, "I have to go. It's almost six in the morning."

"Okay, baby, I love you. Call me when you get home."

"Okay, I will."

I made my way home still wide awake. I couldn't sleep. I jumped in the shower to freshen up, and for the first time in forever, I didn't have a motorcycle on my mind. All that I could think about was each and every scene of that night with

Precious. It replayed over and over and over again in my head until I lost myself to our romance.

Not realizing that I was sitting amongst my kids, I had to snap back into reality. My heart had been there, and my mind and body elsewhere. I'd known Precious for five months, and it seemed we were in this for years. To think of her not being there was like a blazing dagger in my heart; it would be a sore that would forever burn until I could have her back. I wasn't even about to draw that conclusion up in my mind.

I got in my truck and turned some blocks then swung by my brother's house. Truck and the crew were all sitting by the road. As soon as I got out of the truck, he started laughing and shaking his head at me.

"Damn, bro, she must've had you locked down over there. I wake up to take a piss, and your truck was still outside," he said.

"She had me fucked up!" was all that I could say.

"I see," Truck replied, and my phone went off. It was Precious calling as if on cue.

"Monta, I need to see you. We need to talk," she said.

"I'm over Truck's house, baby."

"No, I need you to meet me at the apartment."

"Okay, baby. I will be there when you get there."

"I'm coming across the bridge now," she said.

"Baby, I'm leaving now," I told her.

We made it to the apartment at the same time. We went upstairs and sat in the living room. Then, she looked at me and asked the question I had been dreading, "Are you and your wife still together?"

It caught me by surprise, but I looked at her eyes and could see the tears forming.

"No, baby. We are doing the divorce papers now. I don't want no one but you," I said. As I looked into her eyes, I didn't think she believed me. She leaned over, kissed me, stood up, and turned, but I grabbed her hand and pulled her to me.

"Is this the reason you were crying the other night, Precious?"

"Kind of. Monta, I love you. Hell, I'm in love with you, and I have never loved anyone the way I love you. I don't think I will ever love like this again. You have a way of touching a woman like she has never been touched before. Your kisses are so fucking soft and gentle. The way that you look at me just makes me want to eat you up. I don't even want kids, but you got me wanting to have your baby. I'm willing to give everything up for you, but if I'm going to give up everything for you, I need you to be honest with me. Monta, I have never ridden a motorcycle until I met you. I was scared as hell, but you made it feel so comfortable and safe. That's how I feel with you every day like I have no worries in the world. I don't ever want to lose you, but if you're going to play with my heart, I will have to let go. Do you know how painful that is to say?"

"Precious, you are the flow to my veins. There is no way I would ever break your heart. That's not my plan. My promise is to love you and care for you for the rest of our lives. When you came into my life, you brought the joy I have been looking for all my years. A smile I never knew existed. Do you think I would be foolish enough to let that go or even push it away?"

"Well, I hope not. I would give you some, but my pussy is still swollen and sore from this morning. Hell, I can't even wipe for real," she said, laughing.

"Poor baby. I'm so sorry. I will be careful next time. Do you want to go riding? I can get Truck's seat, and we can ride my bike."

"Sure, I would love that."

"Precious, I love you."

"I love you, too, Monta."

We went back to my brother's house. I pulled the bike out and wiped it down so we could hit a few blocks. It was sunny and warm, and a nice ride through the countryside to smell the flowers and the sweetness of the kudzu vines would be awesome.

As we rode that day, it was like the beginning of a beautiful marriage that hadn't even begun. The sun started falling, and darkness was overtaking the sky. We headed back to my brother's house and gave our goodnight kisses before she drove away. I felt a lonely spot in my heart as she pulled out of the yard.

Why? I had no idea, but it was a strange feeling. I thought no more about it and hung out with the guys. In the back of my mind, my thoughts flipped all kinds of ways.

As the night went on, the guys and I talked, tripping out as always until Ry pulled up out of nowhere. We all looked at each other like, *"What is she doing here?"* Then, we went on talking, not thinking anything about her. Eventually, everybody started breaking off to go home.

"I'll see you tomorrow," I told Truck and headed to the house.

When I pulled in the yard, I sat there for a minute, and I just happened to look up and see Ry's car ride by. I put two and two together, went into the house, and got ready for work. I texted Precious goodnight and told her I loved her, but I didn't receive a text back, which was unusual.

I got in bed and quickly fell asleep. Before I knew it, it was 5 a.m. I jumped out of bed and headed out the door. Like always, I sent my "Good morning beautiful" text to Precious. Once again, there was no response. I was halfway through my workday when I got a text that said: *Oh hey!*

Knowing that couldn't be my baby, I just continued working. As soon as I hit the clock, I called Precious but got no answer. I texted her, and ten minutes later, she texted back: *I'm at work.*

Me: I need to see you when you get off.

When 10 p.m. rolled around, she texted me and told me to come to her job. I headed over to her job and parked. She came out, jumped in the truck, and I could tell that something was off with us. Still, that 'hey baby, I miss you kiss' remained the same. Not one to beat around the bush, I asked, "What's going on with us? Why are you so distant today?"

Her eyes teared up. "I know you and your wife are still together!" she said.

I dropped my head before looking into her eyes. "Baby, when we had our talk the other day, I told you we weren't together. We are doing our divorce paperwork, and I'm not playing. Like I told you then, I wouldn't do anything to hurt or push you away. I still stand on those words. Precious, you are my best friend. If it's anything you want or need to know, please just ask me. To you, I'm an open book. For the first time in my life, I can say that to a woman. I will never keep anything from you."

"Do you promise?" she asked.

"Baby, I promise to never keep you in the dark about anything. When I told you I wanted to make this forever, that wasn't a joke."

"Well, can I come over when you get off tomorrow?"

"Baby, you don't have to ask me that. Do you want a key? I will go get you one made tomorrow."

"Okay. Thanks, babe. I would love to have a key. I will see you tomorrow, and Monta, please don't break my heart."

"I won't, baby. I promise."

I headed back to Truck's house, and we sat out there for a while. Then I went home to get ready for work the next day. As I laid down for the night, my thoughts wouldn't let me sleep. It was like deep down I knew she was slowly slipping away, and I already knew the issue. All that I could do was just hope she saw it too.

Chapter Four

I woke up to my alarm clock blaring. My phone was lit up, and I could see that I had ten missed calls. I hurried up and unlocked my phone, thinking it was my baby, but it was an old ex. Knowing her history of trying to track me down, I wasn't even going to bother calling back or responding to her messages. I got ready for work and left home prepared to get this day over with. I texted my baby *Good morning* and *I love* you so that when she woke up, she would see my thoughts for her like every other morning.

As soon as I sent the text, I got one back saying: *Good morning handsome. I can't wait to spend time with you today!*

Me: I know beautiful. I can't wait myself.

Precious: So Monta, what if I get pregnant? Then what?

Me: Baby you pop a pill faithfully so you won't.

Precious: But what if I don't take one, and I want to get pregnant?

Me: Then we would cross that road when or if we ever get there my luv. But know I have your back through any and everything!

Precious: Ok handsome. I will talk to you later!

Me: Ok beautiful. When I get off I'm going to get your key made. Then I will be at the house.

Time went by slow that day. It just seemed like 5 p.m. would never get here. The clock was stuck on 4:30 for hours. A driver pulled his truck in needing three tires, and I could have kicked his ass. I was ready to go, but me and my coworker, Chris, got to it and by 5:15 p.m. we were walking out the door. I hurried to the house, showered, and put on some fresh clothes. I went to Marvin's, got Precious's key made, and headed to the apartment to wait for her.

"Hey, baby. I'm on my way to the house, so meet me there," I told Precious when I called her. She was turning the corner by the time I parked my car.

We sat outside for a while, talking before we went upstairs. My cousins were in the living room high as hell. One was comatose, and the other was cleaning the same spot for five minutes. We laughed at them for about thirty minutes, then went to my room. Before I could turn around to embrace her, she jumped into my arms. She started kissing, biting, and sucking my neck. Precious just took control for a little while before the Mandingo in me kicked in.

Someone knocked on the front door as I was sliding inside of her, but we were still in our zone, so we ignored the knocking until it got louder. I could tell my cousins' high had fallen, and they sounded pissed when they called out, "Who the fuck is it?"

The shattered voice outside was none other than Shevonne's. Yo-yo called out, "Shevonne wants you, Monta!"

"Tell her I'm not here," I said.

Precious and me hadn't missed a beat. We were still going at it; she was all over me as she exploded and got soaking wet. She started biting on my ear, saying, "Go deeper, baby, deeper! Tonight, I don't care about the pain. I just want to feel you inside me. Damn, baby, I'm cumming again. Shit, what are you doing to me, Monta?"

I could feel her body quiver and shake under me like she was losing control. Then, H Town's "Knockin' Da Boots" came on, and the house just went into outer space. Every time I stroked, she came repeatedly, quivering as she let go. Her legs flapped, shook, and shivered. Her eyes rolled into the back of her head. The slower I stroked and the deeper that I went, the more she gave it up.

Knowing she had nothing left in her, I gave her that 'I can't leave this man dick,' and it woke her back up. The way she was cumming and shaking, I thought I was on a volcano for a minute. As our lovemaking got more intense, she wrapped her legs around me and said, "Baby, let's cum together." I wasn't ready yet, but as she reached her peak, I made it my business to grant her wish. I let go, and she let go, then we let go. I wasn't finished, so I flipped her over and kissed her on the neck, jump-starting her body once again. She trembled and looked back at me.

"Put it in, and let me do the work for you," she moaned out. As soon as she said that, Tank started playing. She put her head down, and slowly, she lost her mind. In all my years on this Earth, I had never felt or seen a body move like that. She looked back again and said, "You taught me everything. Now grade me, teacher."

With everything in me, I screamed, "A-plus." The way she was rolling that ass, she knew how to make me explode. When it reached the tip, and I came, I screamed again, "You passed."

She laughed, but I was too weak to move. That night would be one to remember. I couldn't move, and she couldn't walk. She looked at me and said, "I'm tired of going home and can't walk." All that we could do was laugh.

I got up to go to the bathroom, and she jumped. "Your cousins are in there," she said. I heard them when they left, so I opened the door, smiling. Precious climbed under the covers saying, "Close the door!"

Shaking my head, I said, "Come on, baby. They left thirty minutes ago."

We cleaned up and headed down the steps. When we opened the door, I noticed that my clothes and shoes were in bags at the door. I assumed that was what Shevonne had come over to bring. I stepped over them and walked Precious to her car, gave her the key, and kissed her goodnight. I put my things upstairs and headed to the house because I had a long day ahead of me the next day. I texted my baby and asked her, "Will I see you tomorrow?"

She said, "I will come over after the game."

We said our usual "I love you and goodnights" and I got home to the house I still shared with Shevonne, showered, and went to bed. I was thinking I was going to get some rest, but that was out the window. I laid awake most of the night, and it wasn't long before my clock was going off. I went to work with no sleep, but knowing I was going to see my baby soon helped me make it through the day.

Good morning handsome, Precious texted me before I could text her.

Me: So baby, you're up early I see

Precious: I couldn't sleep baby. Thinking about you and our night kept me up!

Me: I didn't sleep myself, baby. I'm about to go upstairs and go to sleep in this bathroom!

Precious: Really Monta?

Me: Yep really.

Precious: Well, I will see you tonight then baby. Ok handsome?

Me: Ok beautiful. I love you!

Precious: I love you too!

We texted throughout the day, and 5:00 finally came. I went home, showered, got dressed, and went to Truck's house for a while. Then, I went to the apartment and waited for my baby to come over. I waited for three hours, and then I called her and got no answer. I texted her, and there was no answer, so I waited for another hour and called back. No answer. I texted again and got no response. Finally, I got a call from her phone, but it wasn't her. Some female said, "Precious said she isn't coming."

"Tell her to tell me that," I said, and the phone hung up.

That was the night I found out who Anthony Hamilton was. I listened to him for hours until I pulled myself together and sent Precious a long text, letting her know how I felt. I told her whenever she was ready to talk she had my number. I went home knowing there wasn't going to be any sleep going on until I spoke to Precious again. My eyes couldn't close; it felt like I had no breath to breathe. The love of my life was slipping through my hands.

My Saturdays weren't the same. The sun didn't shine the same. The wind blew a different way. When the rooster crowed, it sounded as if it was laughing at me. I thought riding my bike would make it better, but when I twisted the throttle, I didn't feel her arms around me. That only made it worse, so I parked the bike, got in my truck, and went to the projects. I thought hanging where I wouldn't see her would make it better, but low and behold, Precious bent the corner. She saw me and waved for me to come over. I couldn't set my heart or feelings up like that, so I pretended I didn't see her.

Precious stood there until I looked at her, holding up traffic and all. I walked over to the car, and she said, "Get in." I hopped in, and we went around the corner and talked for a while. I went back to my truck and started to open the door. Precious looked at me and said, "So I don't get a kiss? I mean, like nothing has happened!" In her mind, going silent on me was alright. I leaned over and gave her a kiss. She looked me in the eye and said, "You better not be giving these bitches my dick!"

I said to myself, *You gave your dick away so you can't say what not to give away.* But to her, I said, "Baby, this belongs to you." I got out of the car and hung out with my homegirl, Sway. We sat on her porch, talking and tripping out. Across the way, I saw this little fly New Orleans chick wearing some white pants and a pink shirt.

"Who is she?" I asked Sway.

"Oh, that's my friend, Ash," Sway said.

"Call her over, so I can get at her," I said.

Sway called out for Ash, and she came walking over with the sexiest strut ever. She stepped up, and before she could say anything, I introduced myself and held my hand out.

Ash grabbed my hand, and I said, "Hello Ash. It's nice to meet you."

She smiled and said, "I love your confidence, and then you're a gentleman. Damn, everything else your city has to offer is second hand to you. Now, this is the top of the line right here, Sway. You could've been introduced me to him!"

Sway said, "That's the one that be riding the black bike you always be asking me about."

"Oh, okay. So now I finally see the man behind the helmet, and damn, you're fine! So when can you ride me on your bike?" Ash asked.

"Whenever you want me to," I said.

"Hell, you was riding the little skinny white girl on your bike," Ash commented.

"She's not white," I said defensively.

"Well, she looks like she's white," Ash replied.

"That was her who just put me out a few minutes ago," I said.

"Oh, it was? And she rolling up in my hood like that? So are you still with her?"

"Sadly, no, but we are still cool."

"Well, can we be cool, too?"

"Yeah, that can work. So, what are you doing later on?"

"Nothing really. Might be over here with Sway," Ash said.

"Well, put some clothes on, and let me show you something real and get to know you better," I said.

"That sounds good to me," Ash said with a big smile.

I headed to Truck's house, and the yard was full as always. They were cooking up a race, and I was about to add some heat to the pot. I hadn't had a good street race in a while. The Brooks boys had a new bike and wanted to race. They asked me to set them out five bike links and let them spray while I run on motor. For some reason, that day, I was feeling generous, so I gave them ten bikes and told them I would leave after they left.

We got the pot up and went to the spot. They marked the bikes off, did their burnout, and I did mine. The flagman checked both racers and dropped his hand. I sat there until my brother told me to go. When I cracked that throttle, it felt like someone had shot me out of a cannon. My bike literally spun to him in first gear. By the time I went to second gear, I was looking back at him. I had put six bikes between us when I went across the finish line.

That was the day Boo Boo saw what our bikes really had. He looked my bike up and down and shook his head. "It's no way in hell you should have ran him down. He had at least fifteen bikes on you, and then he sprayed the bike," said Boo Boo.

Truck answered, "That's what you call real horsepower."

We all went back to Truck's house and paid everybody that had a hand in the pot. I put the bike up and went to the house so I could get ready for my date. I ironed my clothes, showered, dressed, and dashed myself with some Polo. I was smelling like a million bucks with my Prada shades on.

As I got close to my date's house, I called her to tell her I was near and to be standing outside, so we could make it on time. I pulled up and saw this little, hot, young tender standing on her porch looking down. She was checking herself out. From my standpoint, she was a winning ten. I opened the door for her, helping her get in the truck like a gentleman should. As I closed the door, she looked at me and said, "My night has already started out great."

I had Keith Sweat blowing out of the fifteens in the trunk. That slow melody coming out of my tweeters set the mood just right. She was feeling it from the way she bit her lips and turned her body towards me to strike up a conversation. As she talked, her hands eased over to mine. At that moment, I knew I had her attention.

When I played my cards right, women fell into my hands exactly how I wanted them to. We talked, getting to know each other better like I planned. The conversation was getting so good that we almost missed our exit. I pulled up to LongHorn Steakhouse, opened her door, and helped her out the truck, showing her how she should be treated at all times. The chivalry was so smooth that it caught a few other people's eyes. Guys were mean mugging me because their women couldn't stop admiring my approach.

I only had one person on my mind, and I was pulling her chair out so she could have a seat. The waiter came over to take our drink order and passed me a note with a phone number and a 'call me later' message along with her name. Not to be disrespectful, I ignored it and only focused on Ash. We laughed, had fun, and ate good. I took care of the check, tipped the waitress, and pushed her my number because the whole night she was asking for my attention with that sweet, innocent smile. I told the waitress to call me as Ash walked out the door ahead of me.

I led Ash to the truck, opened her door, helped her in, and we headed to the movies. We didn't watch five minutes of the movie. Instead, we talked, getting to know each other more. Ash told me deep secrets, and I talked to her about Precious, how our breakup started, and the way I felt about it. Before we knew it, the movie credits were running. We headed back down the road, still getting to know each other. She asked me, "What do you want in a woman?"

I had to be honest and let her know I wasn't trying to start anything but a friendship-based relationship until after I got the divorce over with. "Anything else would only lead to more hurt," I told her.

Like a real woman, she understood and respected my decision, but that didn't stop our night. We made our way back to her place and sat in the truck talking and tripping out. We enjoyed the quiet night air with my moon roof back. As time rolled away, our night came to an end, and we said our goodnights. I gave her a friendly hug, and as I pulled away, her lips met mine.

Knowing the touch of my lips would put a woman in her feelings, I slid my tongue across her bottom lip. At that moment, she knew she'd just fucked up because I could feel her body tremble. Instead of taking it deeper, I pulled away and said goodnight again and got out to open her door. I helped her out and walked her to the door, making sure she got into the house safely.

That night, I didn't get any sleep. Ash and I texted all night long, and before I knew it, 6 a.m. was approaching. I got on up and started breakfast, fed the kids, and got us ready for church.

Church flew by that day. I had enjoyed my night with Ash, but my heart was still with Precious. It was like I couldn't shake the hurt and pain of losing her so suddenly. I went home after church, changed clothes, and headed to Truck's house. I pulled my bike out, cleaned it up, and hit some blocks.

As I turned down MLK, I ran into the love of my life. The scene was like a slow-motion film. Our eyes met, and I could see her thoughts, and she could see mine. There was no longer an us, so I just kept it moving. I knew she noticed the helmet on the back of the bike because, as I passed my sister's house, my phone started burning my leg.

I pulled over and answered my phone. The anger in Precious's little soft voice was cute as she screamed, "Who you about to ride on my bike? Don't nobody ass belong back there but mine."

All I could do was laugh, and that made her even hotter with me. "Just a friend. You should remember that we are not together anymore by your request. Right?"

"Monta, I never said I didn't want you!"

"You right. You didn't. Your actions did it for you, Precious. I love you, and I will talk to you later," I said.

As I was hanging up the phone, I could hear her saying, "I'm going to find you!"

I turned down Apple Street and headed to Ash's house. It was like she knew the sound of my pipe coming across the hill because she was standing by the road smiling when I went around the corner. I got off the bike, and Ash hugged my neck. I helped her put the helmet on and helped her on the bike and off we went.

We rode for hours and hours, but it just didn't feel the same having someone else on the back of the bike. Precious knew how to embrace the ride. She knew to lay on my back when I grabbed her hand and pulled. She knew the flow of my body in every curve we came upon. She knew how to tap me to motion for me to speed up. She also knew how to rub my abs to tell me that's fast enough and to cruise right here. I had to learn that every woman wasn't going to be Precious. I would search until I found the right one, or until I got my baby back.

We stopped by the lake as we walked and talked. We played with the ducks and watched the water flow as they opened the flood gates. I could tell that kind of bothered Ash because of what they just went through, so I held her hand as we walked away. She started telling me about her experience with the Katrina storm and how they ended up in West Point. As I watched her eyes tear up, I changed the subject and led her back towards the bike.

Clouds formed in the sky, and it began to smell like rain. Knowing we wouldn't make it to her house before the bottom fell out, I pulled her toward me. I wrapped her arms tightly around me and became one with the road. We made it to my brother's house just in time. As I was rolling the bike in the garage, the sky opened up. We all sat in the garage tripping out. She fit in like she was one of the guys, and from that day on, we didn't go anywhere without Ash.

The rain cleared up, and night fell. I took her home, and she asked me to come in. I didn't want her to look at me like another dude that was trying to get in her pants. I told her I would chill another time. She said, "Okay, I respect that."

I went home, showered, and got ready for bed. I sent Precious a *Goodnight* and *I love you* text, knowing she was probably asleep. As I laid down, she texted back. *I love you too Monta. Goodnight!* The smile that text created was calming, and it put me to sleep.

Chapter Five

My alarm had me up and at it the next morning. I jumped out of bed and was off to work, ready to get this day over already. I sent my baby a text saying, *Good morning, I love you,* and told her to have a nice day. Shortly afterward, she responded. Still not understanding what went wrong, I went on about my day. Ash and I texted back and forth, making plans to hang out after work. My mind still wasn't clear on what went wrong with Precious and me. I texted her and asked what the problem with us was. *Why did you just fade away on me when we were perfect as a couple and best friends?*

Precious replied with some shocking news that made me flip out. She said Shevonne had gotten into my phone one night and texted her. I apologized and let her know I would handle it. My day couldn't go by fast enough. When it was finally 5 p.m., I rushed home. I walked in the house and heard Shevonne on the phone laughing her ass off as she talked to the person who put us on this divorce journey.

I told her, "Hang up the phone and let me talk to you for a moment."

Shevonne hung up the phone, and I proceeded to ask her why she went into my phone and texted Precious. She looked at me with hell in her eyes. "Because I wanted to!" she said as if she had a right to still check up on me.

I was angry, but I went and took a shower and headed to my brother's house. We sat outside on the trailer and talked about the situation. Truck told me that I really needed to slow down. "Monta, you know you're my brother, and I got your back, but you are really playing a dangerous game. Maybe you should slow down with the women until after you and Shevonne are really divorced and living apart."

My phone rang, and it was Ash calling. "Can I lay in your arms tonight?" she asked as soon as I took the call.

Right away, I said, "I would really love that!"

My brother and I continued our conversation.

"I hear you, Truck, but today won't be the day," I said.

We laughed it off, and after a few hours, he had to go in the house and cook the girls something to eat. I went to Spectrum to grab something to drink and ran into the sexiest little redbone. Her name was Low, and we chopped it up for a while.

She said, "I'm waiting on someone, but you can call me so we can get together sometime."

We exchanged numbers, and I headed back to my brother's house for a while until I went to pick up Ash. She was waiting at the base of her steps when I pulled up.

Ash didn't even give me time to open her door. She jumped into the truck. We went to the apartment and up the steps to the bedroom. She told me about her day, and I told her about mine. Then, she leaned over and kissed me. As I went in to seal the deal, her phone went off. She pulled me on down and said, "Fuck that phone. I need you!"

I was putting her into a sunken place when her phone rang repeatedly. I had her under my powers, so she didn't notice it ringing.

"Answer your phone," I said, snapping her out of the sunken place.

After she took the call, Ash looked at me and sighed. "Baby, we need to go to Wal-Mart to get my baby some pampers."

We got dressed and headed to Wal-Mart. All I could think about was how good she smelled and sexy she looked laying there under me. We took the pampers to her sister, headed back to the apartment, and created the same scene. The touch of my lips was like reaching for the clouds; it always took a woman's breath away. As I traced her breasts with my tongue, I could feel her body exhale and go into shock with every graze. As soon as I took control of her legs, her phone rang again.

"What the fuck!" she screamed as she answered the phone.

That time, her sister had called because the baby wouldn't stop crying. We got up and headed over to her house so she could put the baby to sleep.

"I'll stay in the truck until you get the baby to sleep," I told her.

When her baby was asleep, we went back to the apartment. She laid on my chest and waited to see if she would get any more calls. The next thing we knew, it was 5 a.m., and I was going to be late for work. I offered for her to stay, but she said she would rather go home. I took her home and told her, "Tell your sister I'm going to kick her ass."

She laughed, and I kissed her and headed to the house.

I ran into the house, jumped in the shower, got dressed, and headed to work. My workday went pretty smooth with Ash and I talking the whole day. We laughed and tripped out about last night. When 5:00 rolled around, I headed to the house, showered, and got dressed.

My brother called and asked me to drive him to Atlanta to take his bike to the shop. I headed over to his house, and we loaded the bike up, hooked to the trailer, and went up the road. As we unloaded the bike, I saw this sexy ass cougar walk out the shop. I looked at her, and she looked back. We exchanged glances. As my brother pushed the bike into the shop, I stood outside talking with her.

"What's your name?" I asked.

"Nora," she said with a smile.

"Well hi, Nora. I'm Monta. How are you doing today?"

"I was fine until my tire went flat on my bike."

"So you ride bikes, huh?"

"Yes, I'm in a bike club."

"That's great. I would love to see you on a bike."

"Maybe you can. That's if you want to."

"I would love to."

"I stay up the street. Do you think you could come to get my bike and bring it back to the shop for me?"

"Yes, ma'am. Let me go get my brother."

"Okay. I will just wait for you out here," she said.

I rushed into the shop and told Truck that Nora wanted me to bring her bike back to the shop.

"Hold up. I will go with you. She might try to kidnap you," Truck said, and all I could do was laugh.

We followed Nora up the street to a nice neighborhood. I backed the trailer into the yard, and we loaded her bike up and locked it down. She followed us back to the shop where we unloaded her bike and pushed it into the shop. We said our goodbyes and headed back down the road.

My brother looked over at me and said, "Boy, you hell!"

"Truck, until I find me another Precious, I'm going to be on the hunt. Everything that comes my way, I'm going to attack it."

Truck looked at me and said, "Hell, I see."

By the time we reached the first LaGrange exit, Ash was calling me. She was asking me to stop by. We got off our exit, and I told my brother to stop by her house. Ash jumped in the truck with us. We went to the house, dropped the trailer, and went to the apartment.

YoYo was grilling out, so we just chilled at the house and tripped out. As the night went on, Nora texted and asked me to come up Saturday to hang out with her. I said yes, of course. We all left the spot. I took Ash home and headed to the house because I had an early morning. After showering and laying down, my baby texted me to say goodnight. Precious and I texted back and forth for a while, said our goodnights, and I went to sleep.

The next day, I called Ash and told her that we were going to Newnan to get some racing gas. By the time I got to her house, she was by the road in her favorite spot. She hopped in, and I went and picked up my brother and some homies. We pulled up to the shop and went inside. A good friend, who I didn't know worked there, walked up to me and hugged me. We talked for a while, and she told me to get whatever I wanted and that she would take care of it. We grabbed a few things and left.

As we were leaving, I stopped by Wal-Mart to get some things before we headed back down the road. Ash pulled me to the side and told me that she wanted some dick tonight and that I'd better give it to her.

With a smile, I said, "No," but she knew I meant "yes."

We finished shopping and headed back down the road. As I was driving, Anthony Hamilton came on and put me in my feelings.

Ash looked at me and asked, "Are you okay?"

Knowing that I wasn't, I said, "Yes. I just had something on my mind."

Once we got back, I had to clear my head alone, just me and the open road. I pulled the bike out and went up 10th Street like I was the only one on the road. I was passing the cops, flipping them bird fingers, and not caring at the moment. I turned around and headed back to the house with my mind clear and body relaxed. When I got back to the house, they were out there shooting paintball guns that they got from Wal-Mart. Truck, Red, Mike, and Ash were all running around like some damn kids.

We chilled and listened to music. As always, Truck and Red thought they had more music than me. I had to pull out the book and show them who the musicking of West Point was. When Ash said she was getting sleepy, we had to end our DJ battle. We went to her house and sat outside talking and making plans for later in the week. I had to go up the road the next day, so I cut the conversation short, kissed her goodnight, and headed home.

When I made it home, I noticed that no one was there. I took my shower, ironed my clothes, and laid down, but something wasn't right about this night. I was alone, and my mind went wild. All that I could think about was Precious—the time we shared, the love we made, and the smiles we created. It had never been so hard for me to shake a person off, but this one was tough. My thoughts always ended up capturing her and our time spent together.

"Please go to sleep brain, and you better not damn dream about her!" I told myself as I finally closed my eyes.

At 12:00, I was awakened by a knock on the door. *Man, I slept too long.* I walked to the door and opened it to find a man trying to sell something. I slammed the door in his face and went to take a shower and get dressed. Nora had called, so I called her back.

"Hello, Monta, what time are you coming?"

"I'm getting dressed now. I'll be leaving shortly."

"Okay. Call me when you are near, okay?"

"Yes, ma'am, I will."

I gassed up and hit the road. In no time, I was getting off of the Union City exit. I called Nora, and she told me to go on to the house and that she would be there shortly. I pulled up, and she pulled in right behind me. She got out and hugged and kissed me on the cheek before we went into the house. She introduced me to her daughters. I thought I needed to be with the daughters because they were closer to my age. One was actually my age.

We sat down and talked for a minute. Nora said that she was hungry and asked if I would like to go to eat somewhere. Being me, I said, "Just show me to your kitchen, and let me cook for you." She sat there watching me as I began to whip up a five-star meal for the ladies with some steamed vegetables, steak, shrimp, and red wine.

When they were finished eating, she pulled me to her room and jumped into the shower. She stepped out wearing a catsuit that drove me crazy. She stepped to me, turned around, dropped down in a split, and said, "I'm about to give you all fifty-five years of this pussy."

I smiled and said, "You don't know who you messing with. When I leave here, I promise that I will have your old ass sucking your thumb."

She pushed me onto the bed and climbed on top of me. Then, she told her CD player to go to disk three. When H-Town came on, I went to work. I flipped her over, snatched that catsuit off, kissed her on the neck, and bit gently on her jaw. I traced the scent of that Love Spell all the way to her breasts, licking around her nipple before I let her feel the tenderness of my lips. Then, I went up to her lips and took her soul with tender kisses until I felt her quiver. I had her attention, so I made a trail down her body, and as I passed her breasts, I got a tad bit aggressive, just to get that reaction I wanted. I went down her body to her belly button, and she arched her back, so I went further down. Knowing I was going to make her old ass lose her mind with that introduction, I turned the radio down so they could hear what I was about to do to their mom. When I slid my tongue across that clit, she squirted, screamed, cried, and begged me to stop.

By that time, I had her on my shoulder pinned to the wall with that monkey grip on her hands and legs as I pulled her down on my tongue, sucking on that clit. I drove her insane with every stroke of my tongue until it was time to make her tap out. I gently laid her down on the bed with her body and legs still shaking. I slapped my dick on her pussy and proceeded to put it in. It was too big for her, so I got that pussy soaked and forced it in.

The screams and cries got louder. Nora pleaded with me to pull some of it out, but I told her, "This is what you asked for. If I come out, I'm leaving." She pulled me down closer to her as her response. Her tears rolled as she sunk her nails into my back, saying, "Go slow. Please, go slow. Don't hurt me. Damn. That hurt so good. I didn't know you were going to be this big. Why won't my legs stop shaking? Why did I squirt like that? I have never done that. What are you doing to me? Please, don't give this dick to nobody else. I'm about to cum again…"

I flipped her on her side and picked her leg up, so I had nothing but control. I slowly shoved my dick in and out of her until she exploded. But that messed up the session because we had to stop. I must've made her slang a rod through her block because, for about twenty-five minutes, she shook and squirted. Every time I touched her, it got worse.

Nora looked at me and asked why I did that to her. I replied, "Because you were talking shit. When I told you I was out of your league, you thought it was funny, so I had to give you something to laugh about."

"But Monta, this isn't funny. You are too big for me. The shit you know, I don't know where you learned that from, but you are lethal! I mean, that shit should come with a warning sticker."

"Well, I won't do it again since I know you can't handle it. Can I at least take a shower in your bathroom?" I asked.

"Only if you let me take one with you."

"Okay, come on."

"You just better not touch me with that thing or your tongue. Hell, I will just let you shower alone," she said.

"Really, Nora? It's not that bad."

"The hell you say. I can't even stand up straight," she replied.

"I'll wash you off. Just get in the shower with me," I told her. I kissed her neck as we stepped into the shower. Then, I pushed her forward, spread them legs, and slid in from the back with slow, gentle strokes.

She cried and creamed all over my dick as the water ran down the crack of her cheeks and dripped on the base of my dick. As it went in and out very smooth and slow, her legs shook from the pressure of the strokes. The deeper I went, the weaker her knees got. She looked back at me and said, "Please cum. I can't take it anymore. If you want to, I will suck it out of you. Just please don't go any deeper!"

"But if you let me go deeper, I will cum quicker," I replied as I went balls deep.

She hit the floor, grabbing her stomach, telling me to just leave her there.

"I will get up in a little while," she mumbled.

I washed off, got out the shower, and put my clothes on. I went into the living room with her daughters and watched TV for a while and then left.

Driving down the road, I got a call from my homegirl, Cole. She was telling me to come by her mom's spot because she was having a little get together. I made it to West Point and went to check the party out, and as soon as I walked in, something caught my eye. I wasn't your average dude, so I didn't flock to a female. I sat back like a lion in his kingdom and watched my prey. I found a spot and just chilled, chopping it up with the whole room.

Out of nowhere, the sexy tender sat in my lap, saying, "I been watching you since you walked through the door. I can see that you are popular. So what's your deal? Who are you, sexy man?"

"Well, I'm Monta, and you are?"

"Monta, my name is Whitney."

"Pleased to meet you, Whitney. You are such a beautiful young lady. So where you from?"

"I'm from Columbus."

"Oh, okay. C-town in the house," I teased.

"And where you from?" she asked. I told her I was from West Point. Then, she wanted to know, "Are you seeing someone?"

"I have a friend, nothing serious. Why? You want me to be your superman or something?" I asked.

"Maybe so or maybe not."

"I think you do. So, Whitney, do you have a contact?"

"For you, Monta, I do. Give me your phone, so I can put it in for you, and make sure you use it, handsome!"

"Oh, I will, but where you going? Sit right here."

She reluctantly said, "I will be right back. I have to dance!"

"You have to dance?"

"Yes, I'm a dancer."

"You're too beautiful to be dancing, sweetheart."

"I know, but I have to take care of my mother and little sister."

"Well, do your thing, baby girl."

"I will be right back! But I'm going to watch you the whole time I'm dancing so no one will touch me," she said.

"Okay, baby, handle your business. Make me lick my lips."

"Oh, believe me. I will!"

I sat there watching her take the men's money while she catered to me. She rolled her hips, and, as she took her clothes off, she walked over and sat in my lap, making love to me in front of the whole room. The crazy part was that I had all my clothes on, but the way she was moving made it look like one of my love scenes.

"Damn, if you can move that good in this environment, I wonder what you can do in a bedroom scene," I said close to her ear.

"Monta, you couldn't handle me."

"Please, don't say that because I take those words to heart."

"Maybe if everything goes well, we will see, huh?"

"Maybe so, but I will make you swallow all of those words," I tried to warn her.

She asked, "So what are you doing when you leave here?"

"Going to the Waffle House. What's on your mind?"

"Well, I wanted to chill with you, but the girls I'm with be ready to go when they are done. We can get together whenever you free."

"That sounds good to me. So I will call you, sweetheart. It was nice to meet you."

"So, you're not going to give me a hug, Monta?"

"Yes, ma'am. I would love to. So, tell me, when I wrap these big arms around you, you're not going to melt, are you?"

"Did you melt when I put this soft ass in your lap?"

"Great point! Well, I will get in touch with you. Be safe going down that road, sweetheart."

"Can I talk to you until I get home so you can know that I'm safe?" she asked.

"Yes, you can do that," I said and headed to the Waffle House to grab me a bite to eat.

As I sat there, Ash walked in, but she was not alone. I spoke, continued with my order, then ate my food, got up, and left. Twenty minutes later, my phone rang. Ash was on the other end, trying to explain herself, but there was no need.

"Remember, we are just friends, Ash. I can't get mad at you, and you can't get mad at me for seeing other people. We do what we want. Okay, sweetheart? I mean, we are still cool," I told her.

A few minutes later, I received another call, and I told Ash, "Hey, look, I will talk to you later. I have another call coming in." I answered the call, and it was Whitney. "Hey, beautiful. You guys on the road already?" I asked.

"Yes, but I wish I could have stayed with you," she said.

"Then, we would have gotten ourselves in some trouble. Don't you think?"

"Well, all trouble isn't bad trouble, sweetheart."

"You're right, but this trouble always becomes bad trouble. I'm mannish, and being around beautiful women like you, I can't control myself, and he can't control himself."

"Who is the other person?" she asked.

"My other head. See, we have separate brains, so that's a hardheaded situation that you might not be able to handle."

"We will see since you're talking all this shit," she challenged me.

"Baby, I promise you I'm not talking shit. I'm just being real."

"So, Monta, what are you doing next Saturday?"

"As of this moment, nothing."

"Well, clear your calendar so I can have your time."

"I can do that," I told her.

"Well, we made it home, Monta. Just call me in the a.m. so we can talk, and maybe you can come to spend the day with me."

"I have to go to church in the morning, but after that I'm free."

"Okay. Well, call me after church then, handsome."

"Okay, sweetheart. Will do! Whitney, I really enjoyed your time tonight if I might say so."

"And I enjoyed you also, Monta! Thank you for coming to my rescue. That was everything I needed. I mean, it felt like we've known each other a lifetime. I was so comfortable with you. When I gave you everybody else's dance, my body connected with your mind, and I heard your thoughts," she admitted.

"Well, then you should have known exactly what I was thinking. I know you felt what I was thinking."

"Oh, yes, I did. I said, 'this man has his arm in his pants,' but then I saw your hands, and that's when I shook my head and said damn!"

"Well, goodnight, beautiful. I will talk to you tomorrow."

My phone went off when I got home, and it was Nora.

"Hey, Monta. What are you doing?"

"Nothing. Just finished ironing my clothes for church tomorrow, and you?"

"I was just laying here thinking about you and our time today."

"Oh, really? And what were your thoughts, Nora?"

"Just how I could get used to you if you wanted to move with me. I mean, you wouldn't have to work. I have my own business so you could become a partner with me."

"That sounds good. If I start a business, it will be of my own creation, but I love the offer. How about you just let me get closer to you, and then we could work out some details?"

She sounded a little disappointed that I didn't jump at her offer, but she said, "Well, that sounds good to me."

"I will call you later, sweetheart," I said, laying down, but my heart and mind wouldn't let me sleep.

All I could do was think of Precious and our time together. No matter how many women I met, I just couldn't shake her. The burning in my heart just couldn't be extinguished. All that I could do was lay there and hope that one day I could wake up next to her. Before I closed my eyes, I texted her goodnight and told her that I loved her. Before I knew it, my alarm was going off for work the next morning.

Chapter Six

Waking up to the smell of breakfast cooking wasn't usual. I walked through the house and saw my first love, my momma, standing in the kitchen. My mom ended up moving in with us to help Shevonne out with the kids since she was working two jobs and going to school.

I went back to my room, put my clothes on, and then got the kids dressed. We all sat at the table and ate breakfast before heading to church. There was something different about church that day. Time went by slowly, but the message was coming for me. The pastor said, "If you love something, let it go, and if it comes back then it was meant for you."

I figured it was best that I let go and just pray about a tender situation. As church ended, we socialized for a while and headed to the house. As I was pulling in the yard, Nora texted me while Whitney was calling. I answered the phone and was texting Nora while conversing with Whitney.

Whitney and I made plans to hang out, so I went into the house, changed clothes, and headed to Columbus. Not knowing what I was walking into, I had every pistol and assault rifle I owned with me. I approached her house and saw her standing outside, waiting, and smiling. When I stepped out of the truck, she jumped in my arms and kissed me like she had been waiting on me for years. We went inside her house, and she introduced me to her mom and sister. We sat around talking before we went out to eat. As we were riding down the road, she looked at me and said, "Thank you, Monta!"

"What are you thanking me for, sweetheart?" I asked.

"For being such an understanding person. I have never let anyone meet my mom or sister, let alone know where I live. The way you came in and laughed and talked to them like you have known them forever shows me that you are an amazing person, and I just met you. So, that's why I thanked you, and I hope I can continue to thank you for a long time."

"Oh, really?"

"Yes, handsome, really. You just made my sister and my mom smile."

"Did I make you smile?"

"You made me smile last night and all night long. I've never had a man that looked at me and didn't say something stupid or just wanted to fuck me. I guess because I'm a dancer they think I'm free or just easy, but I'm not. I have been saving myself for my husband, and until I find him, I will forever be untouched."

"That's great. I'm proud of you. Keep doing that because that's all these dudes want, and then they want nothing else to do with you. That's what I tell my daughters all the time. Be careful of who you let smile in your face because behind that smile is a strong lie," I said.

"You're right, Monta, but you are so different, and you're real. I noticed that when you first walked in last night. And when I had my conversation with you, it was a whole new vibe from the lame-ass lines I heard all night. You were a gentleman, and you were gentle and smooth with it. One of the other dancers got mad with me because I approached you first, but from knowing your mindset, you would have shot her down from the start. Her and another girl were texting back and forth about me in the car. That's why I called you. If I didn't, I would have beat the shit out of one of them tramps in that car. You kept me smiling and calm."

"I'm glad that you called because I didn't need you fighting. Unless you want to fight with me, but that would be a fun fight," I teased.

"Monta, can I sing you a song?"

"Only if you let me sing one to you."

"Sounds good to me. I wrote this song, and the only people who've heard it is my mom and sisters. It's called "What Took You So Long."

I was amazed as I sat listening to her beautiful voice. "Wow, I'm speechless. I mean, you haven't tried getting you a track together?" I asked after hearing her sing.

"I need someone to help me out."

"I know somebody. When can you do it?"

"Right now."

I told her, "Let's go up by my way, and we can make this happen today."

"You see, that's what I mean. You are an amazing man! I wish I could make you my man."

"Well, what's wrong with your maker?"

"It's nothing wrong with my maker. What's wrong with yours?"

"It's trying to make its way to you."

"Well, it's not moving fast enough," she said.

"Well, I'm going to go ahead and let you know that I'm a hoe," I told her.

"Boy, you crazy!"

"Well, hell, I am! I'm just being honest. You don't believe me, do you?"

"Nope, I don't. You are too genuine to be a hoe, Monta."

"Those are the best kind, the genuine hoes."

"Well, you're about to be my hoe then?"

"I know I can be your man, continue to make you smile, make you my best friend. How would you like that?" I asked her.

"Honestly, I would love it."

I pulled up to Reggie's studio, hopped out and opened the door for Whitney. "So baby, you're about to meet a real musician," I told her as we walked through the door.

"What's good, Reggie? I got you a voice, big guy!"

"Oh, really. So, you can sing?" Reggie asked Whitney with a smile.

"Yes, sir. I can do a little bit," she replied, sounding modest.

"Well, let me hear what you got. Get in the booth." Whitney walked inside of the booth, and Reggie asked her, "What kind of beat you want?"

"Give me a slow, mid-range tempo," she replied.

"Okay. I got one just for you." As Whitney started bellowing out notes, Reggie turned to me. "Man, Monta, where did you find her?"

"Well, Reg, she found me."

"We need to record her. She's not recording with anyone?" he asked.

"Not that I know of. I told her when I heard them vocals that she needs to be in somebody's studio recording!"

"Yeah, we can work with her. I can hook her up with some of the guys, and man, she can make it!" Reggie sounded excited.

"Did you hear that, baby?" she asked, and I could see the excitement all over her beautiful face.

I smiled at her and said, "I told you that if anybody could see it, Reggie could." A few hours later, we were walking out of the studio.

I asked Whitney, "So, how did you feel about that session?"

Whitney smiled. "It felt good to be in a booth and hear my own vocals. I really loved that. Thank you so much, baby. You are awesome! I know we really don't know each other that well, but I can see myself with you for the rest of my life," she said.

"Are you sure about that?" I asked. While I thought it would be nice, the only woman I saw myself spending the rest of my life with was Precious. If I had to wait a lifetime for her, I would.

"So, Monta. Could you see yourself with me?" Whitney asked.

"You are a very awesome young lady Whitney, but I'm going to be real with you. You are a very, very beautiful young lady that has a very bright future ahead of you if you keep your mind on the real prize. That's success, not only for you but for your family."

"You know what, Monta? I never had a man that was real and upfront with me. You are what I have always needed in my life, and again, I thank you for becoming a part of it."

"You don't have to thank me, sweetheart. So what do you want to eat, superstar in the making?" I asked, teasing her.

"I don't know, my future king. Whatever you want to feed me."

"Oh, okay. I got something for you that I know you will like, but first, we have to go to the store. Have you ever had a man cook for you?"

"No, never! You are the first man that ever made me smile this way. Or that showed any kind of interest in me besides trying to get in my pants. Like I always say, I'm more than a pretty face and a fat ass."

"Yes, you are beautiful, but you do have a fat ass, baby; I can't even lie! I mean, *damn!*"

"Monta, you crazy!"

"Yeah, crazy for you. I love seeing you smile with your pretty white teeth, cute dimples, and sexy lips. Let me get this food started before you start acting up."

"I told you I didn't know how to act up. I'm a virgin."

"So, what do you want with someone like me? I'm very experienced, and that's not good for a virgin. I can be bad for your health, Whitney."

"One day, I will see."

"Whitney, you can't leave yourself open like that."

"What you mean, Monta?"

"Come here. Let me show you." I kissed her lips and asked, "What does that feel like?"

"Some soft ass lips. Damn, you made me weak then. Monta, what are you doing?"

"Whatever you want me to do or not to do."

"I'm scared, but if I want anybody to do this, it would be you. Only if you want to marry me, though. Damn, that felt so good!" Whitney said. She closed her eyes as if she were remembering the way my kiss on her lips made her feel.

"But what about the food?" I asked her. "You said you wanted me to cook for you."

"I will be your whole meal and dessert. Where are you taking me?" Whitney asked.

"If you are a virgin, then the shower will be your best friend."

"But I don't have any clean clothes," she said softly.

I kissed the side of her neck as I led her into the bathroom. "Baby, you don't need any clothes for where I'm about to take you."

"Monta, your lips feel so good on my skin."

I turned on the water and waited until it was warm. Whitney stepped into the shower and started to wash her body.

"No, baby, let me wash you. I got this. You just relax," I told her. I began running my hands all over her body. When she was comfortable, I explored the source of the wetness running down her thighs.

"Shit, Monta! Your finger is too big. I told you I was a virgin. Please be gentle with me," she whined.

"Don't worry, baby. Let's leave Earth."

"Damn, please don't make me leave! That feels so good." The way she grabbed my head as I licked her pussy lips, I just knew she had reached space.

I slipped that Trojan on, eased her down, and dried her off. As I took her to the bed, I knew her head was still spinning from that flight I took her on. I laid her down and stuck the head in, playing with the entrance for a while until I broke the tissue. I pushed and pushed inside, feeling her tense up as her tears fell. Her nails buried deep into my shoulders as I put her back on the clouds. I took her right nipple into my mouth, gently stroking my tongue around it as she screamed. Her first nut came with violent shaking, and I pushed more and more dick into her. She came again and again, begging me to never leave her.

I didn't want to be too rough, so I took my time and slow-stroked her tight little pussy. I was opening it up more and more by coaching her through the process. I was gentle as she came and came, and with every nut, I went deeper and deeper. The grip her pussy had on my dick made it difficult to send her soul out of her body. When she creamed and squirted, I went to work.

Going deep and slow, she cried out, and I couldn't feel my body anymore. At that moment, I had to put my seal on it, so I picked her up, pressed her against the wall, and slid her down on my tongue. I watched her legs shake as she screamed, came, shook, moaned, cried, and begged.

When she grabbed my head, I knew it was time to pull back. She let it go, and her body went into shock. I watched her eyes roll to the back of her head, and I lowered her down and slid my dick back in her pussy. I gave her slow, strong strokes every time I went in and out. She came, and when I rolled my hips to go balls deep inside of her, she balled up.

I forgot that she was a virgin and that I couldn't be that rough with her, but she was a real soldier. She said, "Baby, you have to get yours. I mean, you went too deep, but for you, I can and will take that pain. Please, put it back in and be gentle with me."

I turned my playlist on and went to it. Xscape's "Work Me" came on, and to space, we went. The re-introduction was everything. My back wasn't happy because she planted her nails in every inch of it. The deeper we got into it, the more relaxed she got, and the more she liked cumming and squirting. There was something about the way she said my name that made me explode.

As we got cleaned up, we talked, and I cooked her a meal of smothered pork chops, rice and broccoli, and some red wine. She ate, got full, and we watched TV and laughed. Then, I cleaned up so that I could take her back home. When she stood up, her pants were messed up. I knew why, but she didn't, so I washed her clothes and gave her everything she needed to care for herself. It was late, and she had to get back home to her mom and sister. After she put her clothes back on, we headed back down the road.

Knowing I just took her virginity made me feel as if I owed her some kind of loyalty. I'd told her earlier that day to look out for guys like me, but there we were.

"Monta. I know I don't know you that well, but you have my heart and just owned and destroyed my pussy. You were a perfect gentleman with me, and I couldn't have asked for a better partner for my first time. Just promise me that you won't break my heart, please."

"I promise I won't break your heart, sweetheart."

"Please don't, Monta," she begged. "So, where do we go from here? Are we a couple?" she asked.

"Whitney, are you ready to be in a relationship? It's more to it than what we just did," I warned her.

"I know that, but you just took something from me that I had pride in. You did some things to me that people only read about but don't know how to do. You can't teach that shit in a class or nowhere else. I mean, it might not have been special to you, but to me, that was the beginning of forever. I don't want to have two and three partners. I want you to be my first and my only."

"I feel you, sweetheart. Well, we will work on forever, okay?"

"That's all I want."

"And that you deserve, beautiful. Baby, let me get the door for you." I jumped out and went to open the door for Whitney.

"See, that's what I mean. My knight is at hand!"

"And always will be, baby."

"Well, I guess this is goodnight, huh?" she asked, sounding a little sad.

"Yes, ma'am. I have work in the a.m."

"Yeah, you do. I'm sorry I had you tied up so long, handsome, but I just love being around you."

"And I enjoyed your time also, beautiful. Can't wait until I get to be with you again."

"Monta, you gave me a new smile, something to look forward to. Do you understand what that means to a woman? Hell, to me. I'm twenty-three, and I never even knew what love was. If it's anything like what you showed me today, I want it. Hell, I need it."

"Sweetheart, that's just a sample of what love is. You have to be ready for love. It's easy, not hard. It's kind and sweet. We, as people, make love so hard and painful. True love is friendship and, if you can't be friends with your mate, then just forget about love. All you will get is heartache and pain, something you don't want, and you don't deserve."

"Monta, I love you!"

"Whitney, please don't say that. You don't even know me enough to even think that."

"Well, I know all that I need to know for now. That's all that counts."

"Okay, beautiful. I will talk to you later."

"Okay, handsome. Call me when you make it home, please, so I can know you made it."

"I will. Now, go and get you some sleep."

"I will when you call me," she said.

Driving home was a great moment for me. I was alone, so I had time to think. I had three wonderful women at my side, and even though they weren't Precious, they were all great in their own way. Precious was great in every way. She was beautiful, sweet, and loyal. She always had a smile on my face. Sometimes, we don't know how good we have it until what we have is gone.

I hopped off 103, and my phone rang. It was Ash asking if she could see me. Since I was near, I said, "I guess I can stop by for a minute, but not long."

I made it to Ash's house, and she was standing outside. I got out and opened the door for her then got back in the truck. "So, what's up?" I asked.

"Nothing much. Just missing you."

"Oh, really? How are you missing me, and you have a whole friend? Tell me how does that work."

"Monta, I just got a ride. That's all!"

"Oh, really? I mean, it's not a big deal. We are still cool, homie. No hard feelings at all. You feel me?"

"Why are you acting like that? It's not like I'm fucking him if that's what you're thinking!"

"You know what, Ash? That's not my business. Now, I have to go. I have work in the morning!"

"Monta, I want you, so why are you doing me this way?"

"How am I doing you? You walked in the Waffle House with this cat and didn't wave, say hi, or anything for that matter. So, again, how am I doing you? You acted like you didn't know who I was, but that's cool. Keep it like that. You feel me?"

"But, Monta, why?"

"Look, I got to go!"

"So, you not going to give us a chance?" Ash asked.

"I got to go!" I repeated.

"Oh, okay. Well, I guess I'll see you later, Monta. I'm sorry." She finally got out of my car and closed the door.

I headed home, and as soon as I made it to the house, I called Whitney. By no surprise, she was up waiting on my call.

It was great to hear her beautiful voice that was so calming. I asked her, "Baby, why are you still up?"

She replied, "I told you I was going to stay up until you got home."

"Yes, you did, baby. That was so sweet of you to do."

"I would do anything for my man."

"Oh, so we are official now?"

"Yes, we are! I told you since you took my cookies that you were going to be my king. And you're my first too! Oh, you are all mine."

"Yes, ma'am. I hear you, sweetheart. Well, get you some rest, baby. I have to get up in four hours."

"Monta, I really care for you."

"I care for you also, Whitney."

"But, Monta, you don't hear me. I think I'm falling in love with you. The way you made me feel the first time I saw you, from that moment on, the feelings have just gotten better and better and better, especially today! Wow! The way you made me feel today was like real royalty. You were a gentleman from start to finish. You have a big ass dick, but you taught me how to take it, and it hurt so good! I wish we could do it tomorrow, but I have class the rest of the week. On Friday, I'm all yours if you want me."

"Baby, I want you right now, but daddy has work in the morning. I'll text you throughout the day, okay?"

"Okay, Monta. Goodnight, handsome."

"And goodnight to you, as well, beautiful. Sweet kisses." I hung up the phone and got in the shower then got ready for bed. In no time, my alarm clock would be going off.

Chapter Seven

As soon as I got into the truck heading to work, I got a *Good morning handsome* text. I wished it was from Precious, but it wasn't. It was the fresh heart that I had stolen. The beautiful Whitney. Even though she wasn't Precious, she was still a beautiful soul. As the day went on, we talked and talked. I doubted if I even got a little work done, and she couldn't have been paying attention in class.

That day went by so fast that I didn't even notice I was there alone. Everybody was gone, so I clocked out and headed to the house. I showered and then headed to my brother's house, just to keep from arguing with Shevonne, like we seemed to always do. As soon as I reached my brother's house, I get a phone call from Ash asking me to come over so that we could talk. I just wasn't feeling that at the moment. I wanted to take the bike for a ride, so I pulled my bike out and went up 10th Street like I was on the track.

I went through the light, and my bike shut off. When I started it back up, I just knew I had spun a bearing. I called T and told him what was going on, and he told me to get it to him so he could check it out. But I had another plan. I wanted to go faster. I told him what I wanted him to do, and he gave me my price and told me to get it to him.

The very next day, I took the bike up the road to T. I decided that I wanted to stop by and talk to Nora for a minute, so I called her. She told me to go by the house when I was done and that she would be there when she got done at her other location. I dropped the bike off and headed over to her house. When I arrived, I knocked on the door for about five minutes. I started to go back to the truck, but I heard the knob turn.

When the door opened, her daughter was standing there, dripping wet with a towel wrapped around her. I hesitated to go in, but she grabbed my hand and pulled me through the door. "Have a seat. My mom just called and told me you were coming. She should be here in forty-five minutes to an hour. Do you want anything to drink?"

"No, thanks," I said.

She sat on the couch across from me with her legs crossed Indian style. She was showing me all her little shaved pretty Puerto Rican pussy. She knew it was wrong because I was seeing her mom, but she was a year younger than me. She was sitting there looking all good, wet, and beautiful.

As she typed on her laptop, she looked at me and caught my eye. Biting her lip, she set the laptop down and came to sit in my lap. Pressing her breasts in my face, she told me to give her whatever it was that I gave her mom. I pushed her away. I wasn't trying to get caught fucking Nora's daughter. I got up and turned to walk towards the door, but she jumped in front of it. She dropped her towel while grabbing my hand to put it between her legs.

"Do you see how wet you got me? And it's not from my shower either," she said as she jumped into my arms and wrapped her legs around me.

"We have time. My mom won't be here for a while. She slid down and pulled me to her room, pushed me on the bed, and reached in my pants. She jumped when she felt my size.

"We're going to need some lube because that's not going to fit in me."

Knowing we had little time, I picked her up and slammed her on the bed. I spread her legs, stuck my head in, and pushed with a slow stroke. It took a minute to get my head in, but once it made its way through her lips, the rest would be pain and passion.

As I stroked, she cried, "It hurts, but don't stop. Please, don't stop. I'm about to cum." Then, she buried her nails in my back, saying, "Go deeper! Please, let me feel what my momma felt because it took us hours to clean her room up. Make me squirt!"

I pulled out and locked her legs behind her head. I slid my tongue across her clit and sucked on it, then stuck one of my fingers in her pussy and one in her ass. I hit that clit twice with my tongue, and she came and squirted and squirted and creamed. Before she could cum again, I slid my dick back in her and stroked her so hard and strong that she screamed and cried so loud.

We didn't hear Nora walk in the door, but when she walked in, I was on the edge of a nut. She dropped down to her knees, crying while screaming, "Why? Why would you do this to us, Monta? Please, tell me why! That's my daughter, and you are my man! That's my dick, and you just shared it with my daughter."

I didn't want to throw her daughter under the bus, so I just said, "I'm sorry" and got up, put my clothes on, and left.

Heading down 85, my mind was turning flips. My phone went off, and on the other end was a crying lady.

"I'm sorry. I didn't mean to be so upset with you. My daughter told me what happened and that she was sorry. She thanked you for not telling me what really happened. Monta, I'm still hurt because we had something special, and my heart really belonged to you. Now, I know my daughter will lay in her bed at night and think about and dream about you like I do at night. What you give isn't just some normal shit. You give a woman a new meaning of motherfucker. I love you. Feeling the way you make a woman feel isn't normal in any kind of way. I know some other woman may feel that way about you, but now I have to share that feeling with someone in my house! I just hope we look at each other the same as mother and daughter and not 'this chick is on the phone with my man type of way.'"

"Sweetheart, I know you might not want to speak to me ever again. I will at least say that I am sorry, and I hate that happened that way. I hope you can forgive me because you didn't deserve that. I know you need a man that is your age and not your kids' age. I don't think we will work out, so this is goodbye."

"Monta, you can't leave me. I don't want that. I need you. I want you. Will you please come back, so that I can hold you?" Nora pleaded with me.

"No. I don't think that would be a good idea, Nora."

"Well, can I come to you then?"

"If you want to. But it will be next weekend. I have something to do this weekend."

"Oh, okay. Next weekend will work for me. Monta, thanks for being understanding, but know that I'm still hurt. To see you stroking my daughter the way you did me was heartbreaking. It hurt me bad to see my baby in pain like I was in pain. That's something a mother doesn't want to see!"

"Well, sweetheart, we can't think about that right now. All that we need to be focused on is us. Not what happened between your daughter and me."

"You're right. I'm sorry. I didn't mean to get you upset."

"Baby, I'm not upset. I was just saying that talking about it and thinking about it isn't going to make that situation any better. Nor will it make it go away. But if you keep it from your tongue and thoughts, then maybe it will go away."

"No, it won't ever go away. All I was thinking about when you walked out was that I would never see you or feel you again," she said, and I could hear the emotion in her voice.

"But you are baby, so please just let it go. Look, hold on. Let me catch the other end." I clicked over to answer Whitney's call.

"Hey, Monta!"

"Hey, Whitney. What you doing, beautiful?"

"Nothing much. Just finished feeding my sister."

"Oh, okay. Hold on for a minute, baby." I clicked back over to Nora. "Hey, let me call you back. I have an important call on the other end."

"Okay, but please call me back!"

"I will." I flashed back over to Whitney. "Hey, baby. I'm back. So, what did you cook, sweetheart?"

"I just baked some chicken and cooked some corn and rolls."

"Sounds good. Wish I was closer so I could come get me a plate."

"Where are you?"

"I'm coming from Atlanta. I just took my bike up there and dropped it off at the shop."

"Man! I wish I could have taken that trip with you," she replied.

"I wish you could have also, but I'm going back up there this weekend. I have to take a pipe up there and drop it off. You can go if you want to," I told her.

"Really? I would love to. Just let me know what time, and I will be ready."

I asked, "So, baby, what are you about to do?"

She replied, "Shower and get ready for bed."

"Oh, really. You're about to do all of this without me, sweetheart?"

"Well, why don't you come and do all of it with me then?" she asked.

I was tempted to swing through and pick her up, but I said, "Maybe we can do that together this weekend."

"How about we *can* do that this weekend instead of maybe?" she suggested.

"Well, that works for me also. I can't wait to have you in my arms, Whitney."

"I can't wait to be in your arms, Monta."

"How's your sister and mom, sweetheart?"

"They are doing great! My mom asked about you earlier today."

"Oh, she did? And what might I ask did she ask, my love?"

"She just wanted to know what you been up to and how did I feel about you."

"How do you feel about me?"

"Really, Monta? You know how I feel about you. You have my heart. I hardly know you, but I'm falling in love with you. I love the way that you treat me, the way you made my mom laugh, and showed them love. That made my heart cry out for you. My sister had a smile on her face, and it was all because of you. Monta, I want a lifetime of happiness with you if that's not asking too much."

"I would love to share a life with you also, beautiful." I couldn't believe that I was telling Whitney this knowing Precious had my heart. I didn't know why I couldn't shake her. My feet were moving, but my heart and mind just wouldn't let go. I had this woman trying to give me what had been taken away, but I refused to let go of Precious.

"Monta, are you willing to give me your all?" she asked.

"When you say my all, what are you meaning? To be honest, I really like you, but I just can't shake my ex. I mean, you have me physically, but she has everything else. It's like making love to your body, but all I see and feel is her. I'm sorry that it's like that. I don't want to lose you because I love who you are. I enjoy you and your time, but I feel if I can't give you my all, then I'm cheating you out of true love."

"But, Monta, I'm willing to be here with you. I will stand by your side until you can give me your all. Monta, I really don't think you know how much you really mean to me. My mom asked me the other day if you had a gold dick or tongue because she has never seen me act like this before. I wanted to say, 'if you only knew, Momma!' My mom was the only other person that knew I was a virgin. You were the only man that I let come close to even being in a room alone with me. I am willing to dedicate my life to you in spite of how you feel about her. Please, Monta, let me be a part of you. Let me see the world of you, have your kids, and wake up next to you. Whatever it takes, I will do just to be with you."

"Well, I mean, we can give it a try, but I can't make any promises," I said, honestly.

"I don't want any promises. I want your heart. I know that I want to be in your life, and I will get what I want, or maybe I won't, but I can say this: I tried until there wasn't any more trying left in me. So that should let you know that I will never stop."

"Okay, sweetheart, I hear you. I will talk to you tomorrow. I have to get ready for bed. Goodnight, beautiful."

"Goodnight, handsome!"

I went into the house, got my clothes ready for the next day, and took a shower. Standing in the shower, all I could think about was the hearts I was breaking, trying to get back to Precious. To hear the cry of a searching heart was a little hard tonight. To hear Whitney express her feelings to me in the same way I felt for Precious was difficult. They say, when you are in love, the things you would find yourself doing is limitless. And for the first time ever, I found myself in a place with no hope.

Twenty women wanted me, but my mind was only focused on this special one. Until the day that she walked back into my heart, my cry would continue. Our future might seem surreal, but our yesterday was still alive.

As the water runs down my face and back, I still can't believe your gone. But is it selfish to ask for more when all the times you cried your tears I ignored? I don't know where to start my healing process without your help, Precious, I thought aloud until a knock at the door brought me out of my thoughts. A small voice asked, "Dad, are you okay?"

"Yes, Son, I'm fine!"

I got out of the tub, dried off, and put my clothes on. As I laid down, I prayed for understanding and to have an open and soft heart for all the ladies that I brought hurt and pain to.

Hours later, I was waking up to my alarm. As I dressed for work, my mind was still walking through my late night thoughts. I headed out the door, and my phone buzzed with a text from Whitney sending me a *Good morning* and a kiss.

Me: Good morning beautiful. How are you this morning?

Whitney: I'm ok handsome. Missing you. That's all!

Me: Well you don't have to miss me long. We only have a day and a wake-up, then I will have you next to me. I can't wait!

Whitney: Monta I hope your day is quick and smooth.

Me: I hope your day is as well my love!

My day did go by quick, and as soon as I got off, I headed to the house. I was going to be away for the weekend, so I spent time with my kids. We watched movies and played PS3. As the night went on, we all got ready for bed. My phone went off, and I let it ring for a moment. I didn't know the number, but I finally answered, and a familiar voice said, "Hello. How are you, stranger? I have been waiting on your call."

"Hey, Lo Lo. How are you?"

"I'm good, and you?" she asked.

"Well, I have been great. Just working!"

"So, what are you doing, Monta?"

"Getting ready for bed, and you?"

"I was just sitting here thinking about you."

"Oh, really. So, what were you thinking about me?"

"I was just wondering how you were doing, that's all."

"Well, sweetheart. Everything has been good this way. Now, how about you?"

"Well, I'm still alive."

"You have been doing wonderful yourself also. Every day you get above ground is a blessing, and you have another chance at making it better," I said.

"That is so true! So, Monta, can I see you?"

"Maybe tomorrow, but right now, I'm about to lay it down. I have an early day ahead of me."

"Well, can I see you tomorrow then?" she asked in a soft tone that I couldn't say no to.

"We can arrange that. I get off at five. I have to come home and put some clothes on, and then I will come up your way."

"Okay. That's fine. Just call me, Monta."

"Okay, beautiful. Goodnight."

I lay down, thinking hard about my future and who I wanted to spend it with. At this point, Precious was still the only one I could see myself with. The only one in my vision.

Chapter Eight

My favorite clock woke me up, and with cold in my eyes, I got dressed, washed my face, brushed my teeth, and headed out the door. My day moved pretty quick and smooth. Me and Whitney texted all day, on and off, but my phone was still waiting for the grace of Precious. As I hit the clock and started out the door, my phone went off. Lo was wanting to know what time I was coming up her way.

"I have to go home and shower and put on some clothes. I have oil all over me," I told her.

"I can help clean you if you want me to," she said seductively.

"I would love that, but maybe next time, my love."

"Okay. I will be waiting for you, handsome."

"Okay, sweetheart. I won't have you waiting too long. I promise."

After I showered and was getting dressed, my one and only baby called me out the blue and said she needed some gas money to get back to school. When it came to Precious, no one else mattered, especially with her being in college. She met me at my sister's house, and we sat and talked, laughing and kissing like old times. My heart hadn't been that happy in a while, but if anyone could make it smile, it would be Precious.

It was getting kind of late, and she had to drive back down the road, so I kissed her and let her go reluctantly. To let what my heart had been crying for ride off was the hardest thing I ever had to do. The further Precious got down the road, the more my heart hurt.

I had to pull myself together because my phone was going off. When I looked at it, I had thirty-four missed calls and twenty-five text messages. I answered my ringing phone. On the other end was a very calm voice saying, "Baby, I've been waiting on you to come and get me."

Being the man I am, I didn't lie to her about what I had been doing. She understood so that made me want to pick her up even more. I headed up the road. The entire drive I talked to Whitney until she got tired and fell asleep. Yet, my thoughts couldn't control the situation that Precious brought out of me all over again.

I pulled into Lo's yard and got out of the car. She was sitting on her step, smiling. She jumped up and ran to me, giving me a big hug like she missed me. That night, we just hung out at her house, talking and getting to know each other. When it got late, we said our goodnights. I headed down the road so that I could get ready for work in the morning.

As I pulled into the driveway, Precious called to let me know that she made it to school. That was the perfect moment for me to ask her back into my life and my heart. She said that she would have to think about it, and I couldn't blame her. It was my fault that she went away, but maybe I could have her in my life again one day. Reluctantly, I went into the house, showered, got my work clothes ready, and a bite to eat. Then, I called it a night.

The next morning, I woke up before my alarm could even go off. I was getting ready for work when it hit me that it was Saturday. I texted Whitney, letting her know I would be at her house around 10 a.m. I headed to Waffle House and grabbed a bite to eat before I headed down the road.

Whitney texted me that she was ready and waiting for me. The closer I got to her, the more my heart smiled. My heart only smiled for one woman, and that was Precious, but Whitney had created a smile inside me that was only for her.

As I turned onto her block, I could see her standing at her door, checking herself out. From a distance, I could see all the unique and perfect curves that she possessed. I mean, nothing was out of place. Her smile was like the sun shining down in your face so bright and beautiful. I pulled up and hopped out of the car to go over and open the door. As I held out my hand, she grabbed it like the unique queen she was. It was as if she was used to this type of treatment.

As she proceeded to step into the car, I pulled her in for a deep, passionate kiss. She fell into my arms with a breathtaking smile as if she was living her dream. We got in the car and headed up the road. Knowing I had to go by Keith's to get the pipe, I got off the LaGrange Mall exit while laughing and listening to good music. This was just the moment that a couple wished for.

Before we knew it, we had arrived at Keith's shop. I didn't waste any time going inside to pay Keith for the pipe. I was out the door in no time. I had a lot to do but not enough time in the day to do it. We left Keith's and headed to T's shop. I called T and informed him that I was on my way. He gave me his address and told me to bring it to his house because that's where my bike was.

We arrived at T's house, and he showed me the work he had finished and what all he had left. Then, he invited us in, and we all sat around talking, tripping, and watching time get away from us. I told T to call me when he was done, and that I would come and pick my bike up.

Whitney and I headed to the mall to get something to wear to the party that my cousin was having in Cannonville that night. We went to South Lake Mall to pick up a few things, went to LongHorn Steakhouse to eat, and headed back down the road. Our ride back was kind of quiet until she looked over at me and said, "Baby, can I sit in your lap? I just want to rub my pussy on your dick. She is hot over here, and I can't take it anymore. We are too far away from West Point."

We were coming up on the exit, so I said, "Just hold on, baby. We are five minutes away from the house, but you can pull it out if you want to. She unzipped my pants and pulled out "damage." Then, she said 'hi' to him and began singing into the mic. I could tell it was her first time because, even though she was a singer, she couldn't hold a note that night.

As we pulled in front of the house, the street was dark, and no one was around. I pulled up her skirt and bent her over the hood of my hot car and told her, "Put it in." It took a minute because that kitty was still tight, but she pushed them lips around my head and made that pussy wet. He stretched his way in with the tugging and burning of her tight lips around my dick. I picked her up, turned her around, laid her back on the hood, and spread her legs wide as I slid in.

My hands and her back were burning from the hood of the hot car, but at that moment, we didn't care. She said that she wanted to do it in the shower, so I carried her in the house step by step. It got more intense and wet as we stepped in the shower, clothes and all. That cold water hit her back, and she came repeatedly while asking for more dick. I instructed her that we must go as slow as possible. She turned around and looked me in my eyes, trembling from the pain of the strokes.

Then, she softly said, "Baby, you're a great teacher. Now, teach me how to take it fast, strong, and deep!"

"Are you sure that you want that?" I asked.

"Please, give it to me."

I said, "Close your eyes and grip that pole."

Ready, set, go. Stroke by stroke, I drove dick in and out of her pussy so slow and strong. For step two, my strokes got harder and stronger.

"Now, grip that pole tighter and look back and watch this dick work magic!" I told her.

"Monta, it's too much! I can't take no more!"

"Shhhhh. Now let's move to step three. Give me your hands and scream as loud as you want. I'm about to make you burst a pipe with every stroke. Ask for it harder!"

"But it's going to hurt."

"No, it's not. Just follow my lead. Let's go. Stroke one."

"Damn, Monta! That shit feels so good," she said as the strokes got faster and harder. Her knees got weaker and weaker until she could barely hold herself up.

She begged for more, saying, "Go harder, Daddy! This dick is filling me up. Damn, I'm about to cum!" She screamed and shook, losing the feeling in her legs as she fell while squirting and creaming all over the shower floor.

I wasn't finished with her yet. I grabbed her up and put her on my shoulders and slid her down on my tongue, sucking on her pussy, making her lose her mind. She cried and screamed and squirted, grabbing my head as her legs lost control, and she went into a seizure.

I let her down and started showering. When I finished, she was still on the floor squirting, so I helped her up, washed her off, and carried her to the bedroom. I laid her across the bed, and she looked at me and said, "Monta, I don't want to go there again. I'm not that advanced yet. Please go back to step one until I'm ready for the running steps. You can just make love to me because that other shit is for them pro pussy bitches, not me."

We got dressed and headed to the party. All night long, she held on until a song came on that she was feeling. Then, she got up and danced. Guys would try to dance with her, she would say that she was married and look back at me smiling. To see her have fun made my heart smile, knowing I was going to go back to the house for round two. I just smiled back at her as she shook her ass slowly, turning me on and making the night grow closer and closer to the end for us.

"Hey, I want a drink," she said, so I got her a glass of Hen and Coke on the rocks. We sat and talked about our plans for the next day. She grabbed my hand and said, "Let's go, baby. We can go home and watch TV and enjoy each other."

We headed back to West Point. Being slick, I put on a scary movie and turned off every light in the house when we got there. She didn't like horror movies, so the old 'come close move,' had her head on my shoulder and kissing me on the cheek. She turned my head, kissed my lips, then climbed in my lap. Her kisses got deeper, and she looked me in the eyes. "Baby, please make love to me like you did our first time," she whispered against my lips.

I picked her up, took her to the shower, and steamed the room up. I stepped in the shower and let that steam stimulate her whole body while watching the water roll down through her hills and valleys. As she washed her body down so slow and gentle, she motioned for me to join her. I stepped in, and she started dancing on me and turned around and said, "Now, slide it in, baby."

That wasn't my plan. It was time for me to make her a full-grown woman. I turned her around and kissed her on the neck, rubbing my dick against her pussy and sliding it in. As I pushed, she took a deep breath because that pussy had no stretching room. I bent at the knees and lifted up, pushing dick all in her stomach. With my head rubbing her G-spot, she went into space. The moment her soul left her body, her nails were all in my shoulder. With tears rolling down her face, I watched her first orgasm come. I smacked her on her ass, and she lost it. See, that smack sends an electric shock through a person's body when they're in the midst of a climax.

She trembled as I took her to the bed and laid her down. I wrapped my tongue around her clit, sucking and licking it as I slid my finger in her ass and pussy, making her cum even harder. She started to speak but lost herself in the stars somewhere between, "What are you doing to me?" and "I'm about to squirt baby!"

Before she could, I slid my dick in with force and slow strokes. She scratched and clawed at my back while crying, "Don't stop! Please, don't stop, baby! I can feel it about to burst! I'm about to wet the bed, baby. Shit, Monta! Beat this pussy just not too hard." Her waterfall began, and it made things even better because that pussy opened more, and the music started.

The deeper I went, the higher her notes got. The higher her notes got, the more dick I put in her. We were in the middle of a perfect love scene. The way our bodies moved to the sounds of her moans was a hit song. I flipped her over and made her put an arch in her back and then went into action. The strokes went into grind mode, watching her lovely caramel cheeks spread as I went in and out of her pussy from the back as it creamed more and more.

She looked at me and asked, "How am I doing?"

I went deeper and said, "Damn, baby, you are making a very deep impression."

She started throwing her ass in a circle and made me tap out. Then, she flipped me over, got on top, and did exactly what I taught her. When you make one tap out, then you finish them off.

After our long session, we showered and went to bed. That night, Whitney slept in my arms and held me so tight. The next morning, we got dressed and went to breakfast. She didn't want to go home, but our weekend was long enough. I had work in the a.m., so we ate and went back to the house to get her clothes.

My cousins had made it back to the apartment, and by surprise, they had Ash with them. She looked at me with hell in her eyes. I told Whitney to go grab her bags, and Ash walked up to me and punched the shit out of me. I could see the hurt and anger in her eyes. All I could do was look at her and say I was sorry, even though she was the one that walked into the Waffle House with a cat and acted like I was a stranger. I introduced Whitney to my cousins, and we headed out the door. As we got in the car, Ash looked at me with tears in her eyes.

Heading down the road to take Whitney home, she told me she would love to marry me. That sounded great and all. Though my heart was still with Precious, I wouldn't mind trying to make something special with Whitney. I looked at her and said, "Let me think about that one because you know my situation and who my heart is with."

"Yeah, I know, but I'm here with you right now. Not her. Don't let something good slip away from you while you are trying to catch something that's not trying to be caught. Monta, I love you. No, fuck that, I'm in love with you! You have shown and given me shit in a few weeks that I've been searching for eight of my twenty-three years on this Earth. You made love to me, body, mind, and soul, and you were a gentleman in the process of doing it. You taught me what love is and the steps of passion and pleasure. You took your time with me. Like I always tell you, baby, you are not like anyone I have ever met. Now that I have you, I'm not trying to lose you."

"I know, baby. She's so hard to shake. I know that you are a great person, and you have a great heart. But do you think you're ready for me?" I asked. I was wondering if she completely understood the complicated love situation she was walking into.

"Ready for you? What do you mean, Monta?"

"I have six kids, and that's just one thing. Can you handle me and my kids, plus your mom and sister? See, we all ask for something just because it feels good at the moment. I'm not trying to make excuses; I'm just giving you something real. Don't get me wrong, Whitney. You are an outstanding young lady with so much talent and drive but know where you want to go before you get on the wrong bus. If you still want me, we can make this work."

"Yes, Monta. I want you and everything that you have to offer and everything that comes along with you. I love you so much! I promise not to do anything to hurt you, Monta."

"Whitney, I can really believe that. You are a pure-hearted woman who only wants what's best for you and your family. I see that you would do anything to make sure they are taken care of. I saw that the first night I met you."

"Monta, you know I was scared when I was in there. That was my first night dancing, but when you came in, and I got to know you, I was comfortable. That's why I looked at you and danced. If I had to look at them and do it, I would have lost my mind. I knew I had to do what I had to do to make sure home was taken care of."

"I know, sweetheart. Call me when you get settled in, okay? I have to get up this road."

"Okay, handsome. Hey, Monta?"

"Yeah."

"I really do love you."

"I know you do, beautiful. My feelings are also growing. Don't forget to call me, beautiful."

"I won't, handsome. You just drive careful, okay?"

"I will, baby."

After dropping Whitney off, I headed back to West Point with my mind clouded from our night together. The look on Ash's face did something to my soul. We had our little run-in at the Waffle House, but everything was all good between us since then. I just hoped she didn't let this drive a wedge between us. I made it back to the apartment, and the girls were still there, and so was Ash. She pulled me to the side, asking, "What was up with her being here? Who is she to you, and why is she around?"

"Look, Ash. I really like you and all, but you have to understand where I'm coming from. You walked up in a spot with this cat and looked at me like I was a stranger. No 'hey' or even 'fuck you.' I just charged it to the game and left it at that."

"But I told you, Monta. I just caught a ride there with him. That's all!" Ash explained.

"Yeah, I heard you the first time, but I still don't feel the whole situation," I told her.

"I know how that looked, but it wasn't anything like that, Monta. All I want is another chance. All I do is think about you and the time we shared together. Now you're spending time with that bitch! I started to whip her ass, but I was too hurt to even react."

I asked her, "But why would you do all that? I didn't whip nobody ass that night at the Waffle House, did I?"

"Well, Monta, can I at least spend some time with you? Can you take me home and sit and talk with me?"

"I have to go to work in the morning, but I will take you home." I agreed to take Ash home, and within minutes, we were pulling up to her house.

"So, will you come in for a minute and sit with me?" she asked.

"We can talk out here if you want to talk, Ash."

"Why you can't come in, Monta?"

"I just can't. I mean, I can just go home," I said plainly.

"Why would you do me like that, Monta?"

"I'm not trying to do you anyway. I just don't have time for your games, that's all."

"But, I'm not trying to play games with you, Monta!"

I looked at Ash with all seriousness. "Okay, look, I will just call you, okay? I have to get up in the morning, and it's getting late."

"Okay, Monta. I will just talk to you later."

"You can call. I'm just not trying to be up too late," I told Ash, and she finally got out of the car, so I could head home to get ready for work the next day. As I got close to the house, Lo called asking me to come to see her.

"Baby, I would love to, but it's late, and I have to be up early in the morning. I can come when I get off tomorrow if you want me to, but tonight I just can't make it," I told Lo.

"You promise you will be here tomorrow?" Lo pressed.

"Yes, ma'am. I promise."

"Well, that sounds like a plan then," she said as I made it home.

Chapter Nine

Morning came quick as always. As I was heading out the door, Shevonne said she needed to use the truck, so she took me to work. My day felt odd and slow until around twelve when Shevonne called and said we needed to go sign our divorce papers. It was my lunchtime, so I told her to come and pick me up.

That ride was the longest ride ever. I didn't talk, and neither did Shevonne. This had been a conversation for years, but finally, we were making the right steps to the ending process. It's a sad situation when it comes to the kids, but staying in a broken marriage would be even worse for them. We signed the papers and headed back to my job, and for the rest of the day, I couldn't focus on work. Divorce was what we both wanted, but I couldn't make right of the situation.

My phone went off. It was Whitney on the other end saying, "Hey, Monta. What you doing?"

"Nothing much. Just working, and what you doing, beautiful?"

"Nothing much. Just can't stop throwing up!"

"What's wrong, baby?" I asked.

"Well, let me just send you the picture," she said. There was a brief pause before a text came through on my phone.

"What! You pregnant?" I asked.

"Yes, that's what it says, sir. Monta, please come see me today. I need you. I don't know what to do. I'm twenty-three and have my mom and sister to take care of. What am I going to do with a baby? And I'm trying to get my music career going." She sounded so stressed.

"I will be there when I get off, baby, okay?"

"Okay, baby. Will you bring me something to eat when you come, please? I don't even know how to tell my mom. Every time I have to throw up, I go outside so that she won't hear me."

"Don't worry, baby. We will tell her together. Well, let me call you back, baby. I have to clock out," I told her.

"Don't forget to call me back, either!"

"I'm not, beautiful." I hit the clock, and Shevonne was outside waiting for me. I hopped in the truck and rode in silence.

Shevonne looked at me and asked, "Why didn't you fight for your family?"

"Shevonne, we both did wrong. It was at the point where it was best that we did what we did. I held off for years on making that trip, thinking that things would get better, but they only got worse. Maybe it will change. I mean, maybe we will find ourselves in a better situation later on in life. Then, we could see ourselves as one again, or maybe not. Who knows?"

We made it to the house, and I got ready to head to Columbus. As I made the drive, all kinds of thoughts ran through my head. I knew how to hold myself together, especially for Whitney and her situation. I pulled into her driveway and saw my baby at the back of the house bent over.

Seeing her with tears running down her face broke my heart. She wasn't ready for what she was about to go through. She wasn't even ready to lose her virginity. At the time, I didn't care to think of the risk and position that I might've put her in.

When she looked up and saw me, she ran and fell into my arms, crying like she had just lost a best friend. I helped her in the truck and calmed her down. I let her know I had her back every step of the way and that everything would be okay. We got out of the car and went into the house, and I sat down in the living room while she went to her bedroom and put on some more clothes. I talked with her mom, and being a mother, she knew something was wrong.

"Is everything okay?" Whitney's mother asked.

"We'll talk to you about it when she comes out," I said like the strong man I am. Knowing respect is everything, I made sure I showed it. Whitney walked out of the room and sat down beside me with her head held down and tears still rolling down her face. I grabbed her hand and told her, "Hold your head up, baby. Talk to your mom. She is a very understanding person."

Whitney wiped her face and said, "Momma, I'm pregnant."

Her mom replied, "I knew that when I found seven pregnancy tests with the two blue lines. Whitney, I'm your mom. There's nothing you can hide from me. I'm not upset with you; I'm actually happy I have a grandbaby, and you have a wonderful man at your side. Baby, you will make a great mom, and I know that you will continue going to school and pursuing your music career. I have no doubt in my mind because I know who my baby is and what she is capable of. Hold your head up and keep it up!"

"I love you so much, Mom!"

"And I love you, my beautiful daughter."

"So we are about to go get something to eat, Mom. Do you want anything?" Whitney asked her mother.

"No, baby. You two go and enjoy yourselves," she replied.

"Okay, we will be back, Momma. Love you!"

"I told you she would be understanding," I said to Whitney once we were in the car.

"And you were so right, Monta." Whitney was smiling, and I was glad that she was in a better mood.

"So, what do you want to eat, beautiful?" I asked her.

"I want something light because everything I eat comes right back up."

"Well, let's go to Subway then."

"That's fine. Can we go to the movies too, baby? It's still early."

"Yes, baby. We can do that."

"See, that's why I love you, Monta! You have a heart of gold, and you're sweet and very respectful. I have never seen you get angry. I mean, you be beating my pussy like Congo, but that's a great angry feeling right there."

"That's why your freaky ass pregnant now."

"Freaky? Hell, you took my virginity, so who's the freaky man talking to?"

"Well, see what happened was..."

"You took my virginity. That's what happened. Now, get out, and let's go get my food."

"Hold up now. You and little Pee Wee will be walking y'all ass back home!"

"So, you will make your pregnant lady walk, baby?"

"No, ma'am. You know I wouldn't do my baby like that, but I will make your ass walk."

"Boy, don't play with me. You know you love me!"

"You know what? You're right. I do love you."

The smile on Whitney's face was big and bright when she said, "Wow, Monta! You finally said it. Now, I'm really happy! I have the man of my dreams, and we are becoming a family with our little girl or boy."

I told her, "Baby, it's a boy. Trust me. I'm never wrong when it comes to my kids."

"Monta, do you think your kids will like the baby?"

"Baby, my kids are awesome. They will love him."

"You mean her, don't you?"

"It might be a him and a her. You never know," I said, laughing.

"No, it's not. Hell, this one is going to mess up my stuff, so I know I can't push out two babies!" Whitney laughed.

"Yes, you can. It's not that hard, baby."

"How would you know, Monta? Have you pushed out one before?"

"No, ma'am, but I just know."

"Baby pull over. I feel sick," Whitney said with her voice sounding weak.

"Baby, let's just go back to the house. When you eat that food, it's going to really make you sick. You don't want to be running back and forth during the movie, so we can go later when you're feeling good."

"That's fine, but stop by the store and get me a Sprite, please."

"Okay, baby. I will stop at the store by the house."

"Nooooo!" she screamed. "That's blood central, Monta."

"I don't give a damn if it's water central, sweetheart."

I could see the worry lines on Whitney's forehead when she said, "Baby, don't worry about it. I don't need one that bad."

"Whitney, you don't know who I am, do you? Look in the back seat, baby, and in the dashboard and under your seat and right here under mine."

She searched the different areas I told her to, then looked at me with a confused look on her face. "Monta, why do you have a grenade? And all these guns?"

"I told you I don't travel alone. I don't hang with anyone, but I'm never alone." I pulled into the store's parking lot and got out. I went into the store, got her drink, and came back out without a problem. We headed back to her house, and I walked her in the house and kissed her goodnight.

As I left her house, my phone rang, and it was my mechanic telling me to get some ceramic bearings for my wheels. He also gave me an update on my build, and we hung up. Another call came in from Lo. I didn't want to answer, but I didn't want to dodge her. I picked up, and she asked me what happened. I let her know what went on, and she understood, but I told her I would be up to get her Friday. She agreed, and we hung up. Then, my mind was stuck on who I was going to get the bearings from.

All night and all of the next day, my mind was turning. I ran into an old friend, and he told me I could get GG to order the bearings, so the next day, I called and had GG at G & B Customs order my bearings. He told me they would be there Friday. When Friday came around, my workday went smooth. Around 4:00, I got a phone call from the shop. On the other end was the sweetest voice ever.

"Is this, Monta?" she said.

"Yes, this is him, but who is this?"

"This is April from G & B Customs. Your bearings came in today, and you can come to get them. We will be open until 7:00 today."

"Okay. When I get off, I will be down to get them," I said.

"Okay. I will stay here until you get here," she said, and we hung up.

When 5:00 came, I went home to shower and put my clothes on. I sprayed some Curve and put on my shades. I had a plan, and I had to be dressed for the occasion. I headed to Columbus, and when I pulled up, she was sitting in her car waiting for me. My eyes met hers, and our smiles matched. We talked for a while, and then she handed me the bearings and her phone number, and said, "Call me!"

I smiled as I left and headed to my baby's house since I was already in Columbus. I got a phone call from her, saying she was down my way, so I headed back to West Point. Once there, I stopped by my sister's house, and my baby and brother were sitting on the porch talking.

As I got closer, I could see that beautiful glow she had on her face, but when she smelled me, I saw another side of her that I'd never seen. She yelled and screamed, asking me, "Where have you been? And why were you in Columbus and didn't tell me you were coming?"

I was able to calm Whitney down and take her to the house where we talked and laughed. I fed her, then she fed me. The sun was starting to go down, so I gave her a kiss and sent her home before it got dark. She didn't want to go, but I didn't want her to be out late in her situation. As soon as she left, I went to pick up Lo, and we came back to the house. Lo met my cousins, and they hit it off, so we all sat in the house tripping.

My phone rang, and it was Nora asking if she could come and stay with me for the weekend. I said yes, gave her the address, and told her to come in the morning around 10:00. The girls said they were hungry, so we got in the truck and went to the Waffle House. What a surprise it was to see Ash again with the same guy. We spoke and found a seat, and I enjoyed my meal.

It was late, so the girls and I took Lo home. I got them to drop me off at the house and let them keep my truck. I took a shower and packed my clothes for the weekend before I laid down.

The next morning, I woke up kind of late and had four missed calls. I dressed and called my cousin to come to pick me up. As I stood outside, waiting on YoYo to come to scoop me up, Nora called and said she was passing the last LaGrange exit.

When YoYo got there, we headed to the house. I took my bag upstairs and waited for Nora to show up. YoYo and I were sitting around the house talking about the fun we had last night, and when the next get together was going to be when a horn blew outside. My phone rang at the same time. I looked over the balcony, and there she was. Five feet three inches and one hundred and forty-five pounds of nothing but curves, smiling up at me.

I rushed downstairs and greeted her with a hug and kiss.

"Hey, beautiful. How was your drive?"

"It was great, baby. I didn't go to bed until four this morning," she said.

"Why? What's wrong, baby?"

"Nothing. I just had a lot of work that I had to get done before I came down here."

"Did you get it finished?"

"Yes, I did, baby. I had to because I couldn't miss this time with you. I haven't been able to get you off my mind, and I needed to feel you. If you know what I mean."

"No, I don't know what you mean. Why don't you just go ahead and tell me."

"I want to feel you inside of me, Monta."

"Oh, okay! You want that. I gotcha. We can handle that later on tonight if that's okay with you."

"That will be fine, baby. As long as you send me off to space again, I will be just fine."

"Oh, most definitely! You know how I do, baby."

"Yes, I do, and my baby does also. We got into it because she wanted to come with me, and I told her 'bitch please!' When I was walking out the door, she grabbed me by my hair. I turned around and knocked her ass out."

"Baby, you know that I was wrong for that. If it's going to drive a wedge between you and your daughter, I will just take myself out of the situation," I said. I was regretting that I caused the friction between Nora and her daughter.

"No, Monta. You don't have to do that. Like I told her before I left, she needs to have all of her stuff out when I get back."

"Nora, that's your child."

"She was my child when she fucked my man, but that didn't bother her then. Putting her ass out isn't going to bother me now!" Nora fumed.

"Look, sweetheart. I understand what you are saying, but look at it like this. I'm just a man that might be or might not be here tomorrow, but your daughter is a part of you for the rest of your life."

"You're right, but—"

"There are no buts in this situation, baby. Just call her and talk to her, okay?"

"I will later. But for now, I need all of your attention, Monta."

"Okay. You got it beautiful, but let's go get some breakfast first."

"That sounds good to my stomach right there, Monta. I love you!"

"But how do you know that, Nora? I mean, you don't even know that much about me to say you love me."

"I know how you make me feel. There is something about you that makes a woman lose her all in you and just give it all up, Monta. I make over seven hundred thousand dollars every month. To be with you, I would give you every dime I have just to be in your arms at night."

"Oh, really?"

"Yes, I will!"

"But it's not like that, Nora. You don't have to do all that to be with me. I mean, I'm going to be honest with you. I'm in love with a woman that I can't have because I broke her heart, unintentionally. My everyday thoughts are about her. I go to sleep just to wake up hoping for another chance at her heart. But those chances seem so slim at this point in time."

"See, that's what I love about you, Monta! You are honest and upfront. Even if the truth hurts, it's better than a broken lie. And know that I want to be with you. Even if I have to share you, it will be worth the share. I can promise you that."

I laughed and said, "Well, at the moment, you don't have to share me, so let's eat!"

***

We finished our breakfast, and I took her to the lake. Afterward, we stopped by my sister's house and then went to the apartment to get ready for our date night. Nora stepped out of the house with a dress that made the traffic stop. Her curves started from her feet and made their way up to her hair. She was the finest fifty five year old that I'd ever seen, and I had her on my arm.

We went to dinner and a movie then cruised the city, enjoying each other and the beautiful night that came along with it. I put Keith Sweat in and played "Right and Wrong Way," and the beat took it from there. The deeper the song got, the closer she got to me until her hands were stroking my dick like a masseuse. The tighter her grip got, the faster I drove home.

She jumped in my lap and pulled her panties to the side. She slid my dick in and moved her body like a snake. The windows fogged, and the temperature hand was on hell as she rode and rode my dick. She squirted with every stroke. I was soaked, and she was wet. Just when she thought she had the upper hand of the show, I grabbed her shoulders and pulled her all the way down on it. That's when the tears started rolling.

She cried, "I can't take all of it. Let me pull up some, baby. Please, I'm about to cum. Damn, Monta, this dick is so addictive! Baby, let's get in the shower, please. I want to lose my mind again tonight! But let me have control tonight."

We went up the steps, leaving clothes from the front door to the bathroom. As the steam from the shower put us in ghost mode, the magic started. I pinned her to the wall and started making music. All I could hear her say was, "Oh, shit. Damn. Hell yeah." And then, she went to space as she lost control of herself, creaming, squirting, and calling my name in a foreign language. I had her just where I wanted her, so I put her on my shoulders and went to work. My tongue did paint strokes like I was Picasso. With every stroke, she shook and shivered from the tub to the bedroom.

As I laid her down on the bed, I slid my dick in her tight pussy and moved to the beat. Slow and strong strokes got her clawing my back and neck.

"I can't take it anymore. Please, let's just stop for a minute! No, please don't stop. It hurt so bad, but I can't let you pull out. Baby, go deeper but go slow. Let me cream on your dick! Yeah, daddy, right there. Oh, shit, I'm about to cum, baby. Cum with me."

I pulled out and dropped it in strong as her body shook. She squirted, and I came even harder. Knowing this was going to be our last time, I went in for round two, but this time I had to give her that across 85 beatdown. I flipped her over and made her put an arch in her back. Then, I dove in like a swimmer. I was going so deep I could feel her stomach, and the more she tried to run, the harder I stroked. She screamed and squirted repeatedly.

That night, we fucked up some sheets. With every stroke, she came. I was at that all night flight moment. I was on my second nut, so it was time to seal the deal. I slowed my strokes down but still went balls deep. She tried to push me out until she felt that spot she never felt before. My dick started to swell, and that pussy got tighter, and she came several times. When I saw my opening, I popped that spot and put her to sleep.

I got up, took a shower, cleaned the room up, and left her laid out with her legs open and mouth wide open. My job was done. I gave her that Nyquil Z dick! It worked every time.

The next morning, I was sitting on the bed watching TV when she woke up. She looked over at me and said, "Baby, what did you do to me last night? I have never slept that good."

I said, "I did what you wanted me to do, make you go crazy. But this time with a different dose."

"Man, you are a motherfucker. I swear I have never had anyone do me like you do me. Your dick must have GPS or something. That motherfucker knows where every spot is and how to hit it when it feels like it."

"I just know what I be doing. That's all."

"Yeah, I know that much. I wish I could have it every night."

"So, baby, are you hungry?"

"Yeah, if you're going to feed me some more dick."

"Really, Nora. I want some food, so you better go shower and come on before I leave you."

"Okay. I'm coming, but I still want some."

"So, what do you want to eat?" I asked, ignoring her pleas for more time in bed.

"Let's go to IHOP," she said.

Once dressed, we headed to breakfast. While we were sitting there eating, she got a phone call that was an emergency. Our breakfast was cut short as we headed back to the house, where she grabbed her stuff and left.

I had a lot of daylight left, so I called Whitney and went to spend the day with her. She didn't feel good, so I cooked them dinner. We sat around, watched movies, and tripped out the rest of the day. We really enjoyed our day, but as night fell, my time was coming to an end, so I gave my goodnight kisses and left. As I was getting in the car, my phone rang, and it was April, the girl I met at G & B Customs. We had talked off and on but more off than on.

"What are you doing?" she asked.

"Leaving Columbus," I replied.

"Come by and see me," she said and gave me the address.

I made my way over to her house, and she met me at the door. We went to her room and sat and talked for a while. She leaned over and kissed me. I pulled back, so she pulled my dick out, put a rubber on it, and sat on it. It wouldn't fit, so she got some lube and greased it up and tried it again. That didn't work.

I said, "Let me help you out." I put the head in, and for about thirty minutes, we pushed until it made its way inside.

As I looked into her eyes, I could see the pain that she was in, so I took my time with her. I let her get hers and got up. She wanted me to stay for a while and hold her, but at that point, I wasn't in the holding business. I stayed and talked with her for a while. It was something about her that drew me to her. She wasn't the first white girl I had dated, but she was different than the other ones, so we started hanging out and spending time together.

My marriage was over, so I moved out and got my own spot, and April moved in with me. Our relationship was great. We got along well, but my heart still wasn't healed. I felt like it could rest, though. Whitney and I were still together and going strong, and me and Lo were still talking also. But what Nora and I had was dying out. The flame just wasn't there for me anymore. We talked off and on, but that's as far as it went.

April was everything a man could want. She rode motorcycles, helped work on cars, and helped with anything that I did. That made our bond stronger. You could say she was a safe place, my safe place.

April and Shevonne didn't get along because Shevonne would come over and try to take over. April wasn't afraid of Shevonne. Those two went back and forth for months until one night that will play over and over again in my head. It was the day before my sister had her daughter's birthday party at my dad's house. My baby boy wanted to stay with my mom, so Shevonne left him and our oldest daughter for the night.

The next day rolled around, and I went to work. When I got off, I called Shevonne and asked her did she go pick up the kids. She said no and that my mother, Emma, wanted them to stay.

I said, "Okay." Then, I got ready for bed. I tried to lay down, but my conscience wouldn't let me. It kept saying, "Go get Quay!"

I tossed and turned, got up and fixed myself some cereal. I laid back down, but I still felt a big push in my back. I told April to ride with me to get Quay. We drove to LaGrange, and the drive was calm. My heart was warm, but my body had a funny feeling. We arrived at the house, and I knocked on the door. My mom opened the door and went to lay back down.

"His shoes are in the hallway closet, and you need to whip Brea's ass for being so bad!" she said before she went into her bedroom.

As always, I replied, "You whip her."

She replied with her famous saying, "I don't whip nobody else kids."

"Well, you beat the brakes off me," I told her.

She laughed and said, "Because you mine."

If I had known that would have been my last time seeing my momma alive, I would have laid in her arms like I did as a young boy. God was trying to tell me. That's why he sent me to her to make sure I saw her before he took her from me. I got Quay and asked my mom if she wanted me to lock the door, and she said yes. I locked the door, but before I closed it, for the first time as I was leaving her house, I felt the need to say, "I love you, Momma."

To hear her heart and soul say it back was the best feeling ever. April and I headed back down the road, and I dropped Quay off at home. Ten minutes later, Shevonne came over beating on the door, screaming, "Why did you bring him home at 11:00 at night?"

I didn't feel like arguing, so I just closed the door and turned my phone off. That was at 11:10 p.m. From that time until 3 a.m., my sisters and dad tried calling me, but my phone was off, so they called my cousin who lived across the street. I was dreaming when I heard a loud knock at the door. I jumped up and went to the door. My cousin handed me the phone and said, "Call Toot." I asked her what was wrong, and she repeated, "Just call Toot."

I called my sister, and she told me to come to the hospital. When I asked her what was wrong, she wouldn't tell me. She just said, "Come to the hospital and let April drive."

When we got to the hospital, I saw my sister standing outside crying. I immediately felt my heart in my throat. When I walked in, the nurse already knew who I was. She took me back to a waiting room where my dad, stepmom, and sisters were sitting. My dad looked at me and said, "She's gone."

I looked at him with so many questions running through my mind. "Who's gone?" I asked, but when he said Momma, my life ended. I had lost my best friend to a massive heart attack. The only person who could calm me was gone. In that room full of people, for the first time in my life, I felt alone.

The nurse took us to where my mom was laying. To stand there and watch my superwoman lay on that table was the hardest thing I ever had to do in life. As I stood there begging her to get up, she didn't respond. She just laid there cold and still, with no breath in her body. If I could have hooked my lungs up to hers so that she could breathe again, I would have.

A loud scream and a crying voice so familiar didn't make it any better. Shevonne stepped in all broken up and hurt with tears falling. Her weak voice cried out, "No!"

Not in a million years would I have thought my momma would leave me alone without anyone to turn to or call out to. But on July 31st, she was gone, and I was left broken and confused.

Chapter Ten

As time passed, my heart couldn't feel anymore. Whitney would call, and I would snap at her. I cut Lo off. Nora was out of the picture. For a long time, I just had one woman until I met Ty. We talked, and she wanted to come to stay the night, so I sent April to Columbus, and Ty came down. We hung out, went to the movies, out to eat, and back to the house. I wasn't feeling her, so we laid in bed and talked for a while before we went to sleep.

The next morning, I heard a knock on the door. It was April, and she couldn't get in because I took her key. She went from window to window, knocking and screaming, and then she left. I put Ty out and called April. She came home, and we made up.

A few weeks later, I met Coco. I was really feeling Coco as we talked every day and got closer. One Saturday, she was on her way home. I had sent April to Columbus, and Coco came by. We went riding on the bike, enjoying each other until she had to leave.

I didn't realize I was pushing my comfort zone away until I sent April to Columbus for a weekend, and Coco came down to stay. I cooked dinner, made some drinks, and had the scene set right. Coco told me earlier that week that she had bought a catsuit just for that night. She pulled up and stepped out the car with some white pants on with no underwear. The guys across the street were looking and giving me the thumbs up. We went into the house, laid her bag in the bedroom, and came to sit down on the couch. I fixed her a drink. In the back of my mind, something kept telling me to get up and leave. Ignoring the thought, I stayed.

Five minutes later, I heard a knock at the door. I looked out the window and didn't see anyone, so I opened the door, and there stood Shevonne. She pushed her way in, and her mouth went to work. After she stopped talking, she turned and left. Right behind her was Coco. I was left standing there looking dumb with my mouth on the ground and my dick in my hand. I was speechless. I called Coco and asked her to come back.

She said, "No. I'm not mad at what she said. I'm mad at you because you opened the door. You had everything you needed in the house. Fuck everything else!"

The thought of her with that catsuit on, crawling on my bed, made me madder by the minute. I thought, *Hey, I will just call my baby and tell her to come back home.* I dialed April's number, and she didn't answer. I texted her and got no response, so I called her all night long and got no answer. The next morning, she came home, and we sat down and talked. She looked at me and said, "Monta, I love you so much, but I know you be fucking other women."

I couldn't say anything. I just looked at April for a minute and said, "Fuck that! Where the hell was you last night, and why didn't you answer your phone?"

"I was thinking, and I didn't want to talk to you because I know why you be sending me to Columbus. So I'm moving out, Monta. You have hurt me for the last time. I can't take that hurt anymore. Now, it's time for me to put my heart back together."

Weeks went by, and I met Miya. We talked on the phone for a while, and I asked her out, so we set a date. She came to the house, and we went to LongHorn Steakhouse for dinner and to the movies. The movie we wanted to see had already started. We rode over by the football game and couldn't get in, so we came back down the road. Miya came inside for a while and then left. We talked off and on for a little while, then the conversations stopped.

Then, I met Mekia. She was a lovely young lady, but she still wasn't Precious. She came to visit, and we talked, watched TV, went out, came back, and talked some more. She went to the bathroom, took a shower, and stepped out in some sexy ass boy shorts that made me go into beast mode. I jumped up, swept her off her feet, put R Kelly on with the remote, and went into action.

I could tell she wasn't ready for what I had to offer. Before I could even touch her, she came. I put my condom on and just filled her up with dick. As soon as it went in, she came again repeatedly. I stroked slow and smooth as Sons of Funk's "Pushing Inside of You" came on, and the room went crazy. Her pussy was so tight I could feel my dick ripping her walls.

She cried, but that pain didn't stop her from cumming. She wrapped her legs around me and pulled me on in deeper, and the depth of her ocean pulled every bit of energy out of me.

After that session, we laid around, talking and getting to know more about each other. My phone rang, so I got up to check it. It was Whitney asking if I could come to spend some time with her tomorrow. I told her yes and that I would call her back. By then, she knew I had someone else. I wasn't giving her any time, and we hardly talked, but I still loved her and would do anything she asked. She had a couple of weeks to go before she gave birth to our daughter.

I turned back to Mekia and our conversation. She took my hand, looked me in the eyes, and said, "Monta, you just made me fall in love with you."

I asked, "How did I do that?"

"The way you just made love to me."

"That wasn't making love, sweetheart. If that made you fall in love, then you really couldn't handle the real art."

"Well, show me your real art then, artist."

"Mekia, you're not ready for what I have to offer, sweetheart. I'm trying to save you from a lot of heartache and pain, so please trust me."

"I'm a big girl. I can handle whatever you give me."

"Oh, really? Okay. I gotcha," I said. Dropping the subject, I made us some popcorn, and we talked more. Then, she got up to shower. At that moment, I said, "It's about to go down."

I slipped in the bathroom and stepped in the showers with her. Her body was soapy and wet as I watched the water run down her curves. I picked her up, put her on my shoulders, and began to paint back and forth from the front to the back of her clit. I drew my art, and she squirted, screamed, shook, and cried with her legs tight around my neck and her nails in my back. Mekia lost control of her legs, so I carried her dripping wet body to the bed.

I wasn't done with her yet. I laid her down while still painting. I slipped a finger in her pussy and one in her ass; it was time for her to know what falling in love was. In and out with my fingers, I made love to her pussy and ass. She shook and squirted while screaming and begging, "Please stop. I can't take it anymore!" That was my cue to slide my dick in and start making music. Slow strokes and hard strokes had her legs shaking as she screamed, wet my bed, and scratched my back. "Damn, Monta, you are the best. Please don't go any deeper," she screamed.

I pulled out, and she pulled me back in, begging for more. As I got more in tune with her body, the scene became more and more intense. Our bodies moved to the same beat, and then her soul left her body. The language was out of control, and her squirts were more and more intense. She went into a seizure as she shook, came, and squirted. I pulled out and came on her stomach as she continued shaking and squirting.

I left her on the bed and jumped in the shower, knowing my job was done. I put my clothes on and went to the kitchen. She was still crying and asking me for help, but I ignored her until I finished my drink. Then, I returned to the bedroom with her some water and a towel. She looked at me and said, "You were right. I've never made love and definitely never did that shit before!"

I changed the sheets on my bed while she showered. I was laying down when she got out of the shower and came to lay in my arms. For some reason, that was comforting to me. She was fast asleep in no time, and I followed.

Awaking the next morning, I cooked her breakfast and fed her before she left for home. As she drove away, Whitney called, so I got dressed and headed to Columbus to pick her up. We came back to the house, and she laid in the bed and went to sleep. I cooked her lunch and sat beside her rubbing her stomach as I felt my baby kicking and turning. When Whitney woke up, she started crying and asking me, "Why did you leave me to do this pregnancy alone? Monta, I love you, and you said that you were going to be there!"

"Baby, I have been through a lot in these past few months, but don't worry. I'm here now. Okay, beautiful?"

"That's good because I have something to tell you, Monta."

"What's that, baby?"

"I signed a record deal!"

"Wow, really? I'm proud of you, baby!"

"Monta, I needed and wanted you to be there. When I called, you didn't answer your phone, and you didn't respond to my texts."

"Baby, all that went on in the week that my mom passed."

"So, why didn't you call me and let me know, Monta? I'm your woman, and I would have been there for you, baby. All you had to do was reach out to me. How are you doing? Is everything okay with you?"

"Baby, it's a second-by-second process with a lot of praying, and it still doesn't feel like it's getting any better. Every day, it hurts like it just happened."

"Monta, you have to keep praying and trusting in God. It will get better, I promise you. You have to promise me that you won't shut me out again. That's what I'm here for. I'm more than your woman. Remember that I'm your best friend."

"And you're mine also, beautiful."

"So, what have you been up to, Monta?"

"Nothing much. Just trying to get my mind together, that's all."

"I really missed you and our conversations," she said sadly.

"Whitney, I missed you too. Every day, you were in my thoughts, and every night, you were in my dreams."

"Why didn't you talk to me?"

"It won't happen again; I promise you."

"Well, I hope not because I will be having this little girl in three more weeks, and I'm going to need you by my side."

"I will be right there, baby. I wouldn't miss it for nothing in this world."

"Can I stay with you tonight, Monta? I just need to lay in your arms."

"Yes, baby, you know you can. You don't have to ask me that," I told her, and we talked, laughed, and watched TV, just enjoying each other like old times.

"So, Monta, you know I was thinking about putting the baby up for adoption," Whitney said, and the words came out fast.

"You say what now?"

"It's going to be a family member, so we both will have access to her, Monta. I'm not giving her away with me signing this contract; it's going to be a lot that comes with it. I'll make sure everything is taken care of. All I need for you to do is agree with it."

"I will just take care of her, Whitney. I mean, she is my daughter."

"But, I have already done the paperwork, baby."

"The fuck you did! So you mean to tell me you did all this without my say in it?" I yelled.

"Monta, you left me without a word. I didn't hear from you. If I called, you didn't answer. I had to do what was best for me, my child, and my momma and sister. You gave me your promise that you would be there, but you wasn't! I'm not giving her away or anything. I just need to make sure everything is all taken care of, and I know it will be with my aunt."

"So, what you saying is she wouldn't be taken care of with me?" I asked as I fumed over the decision Whitney had made about our daughter.

"No, Monta, I didn't say that, baby. I know you are a great father, and you would be a greater one for her, but I didn't want to put all of that stress on you."

"You know what, Whitney? I think it's time for me to take you home."

"Really, Monta?"

"Yep, really. I mean, you did this without my input."

"Well, I tried to get in touch with you, but you were ignoring me, remember?" she said.

"I wasn't ignoring you! Like I said, I just had a lot going on at the time, but I understand."

"Baby, please don't do that. Monta, I want to marry you. I'm going to the top, and I want to take you with me. It's all because of you that I was put in this position, so please don't be like that. I need you!"

"Let me be honest with you, Whitney. I have another woman, and she lives with me. Well, not at this moment, but she still has clothes in the closet, so I really think it's time to go. I'm ready when you are!"

"Please, please, Monta. Why are you doing me like this? I gave myself to you, and I have been honest with you, never cheated, and never thought about cheating! How could you, Monta? How? Please tell me what did I do wrong, please!"

"I really don't have nothing to say, just like you gave our daughter up without my say. So, it's nothing left for us to talk about."

The way she broke down and cried hurt me so bad, but I couldn't let her see the pain in my eyes. She laid on the floor and cried for hours, asking me why I would treat her like that. I couldn't say anything. All I could do was sit there and stare at her while asking myself why did I do her that way when she was nothing but perfect to me. I picked her up, carried her to the bed, and laid her down, but she got up and said she was ready to go.

"Whitney, I didn't mean to hurt you, ever. It's nothing I can say or do to change that. All I can say is I'm sorry, and I hope you forgive me."

"Monta, you were my first everything, even my first heartbreak. I can honestly say that I'm in love with you. Nothing you ever gave me or did for me is the reason I love you, but I'm in love with the person you are. That's what took my heart. All I wanted was to lay in your arms tonight. Now, I can't even do that because you held another woman in that bed and on those sheets."

"No, I didn't. Those are new sheets, and the pillows are new. She took all that stuff with her."

"But it don't matter. She laid in that bed, Monta!"

"Look, Whitney, just get your ass in that damn bed, please, baby."

"But why should I, Monta? You don't want me!"

"Whitney, I love you. Nothing or no one would ever change that, and yes, I do want you, but do you still want me?"

"I don't know. Come kiss me and see." I leaned over and kissed her so gently on the lips. She softly said, "Damn, Monta. I have wanted that kiss for so long, and yes, I do want you."

I kissed her neck and on down around her nipples. When I got to her stomach, the baby kicked me as if she was mad at me too. We both laughed. At that moment, I knew where my heart really belonged. I had been neglecting her for the longest, so I laid beside her and held her all night. I couldn't sleep, so I just watched her and played with my baby until she stopped kicking.

The next morning, I was already up serving Whitney breakfast in bed and planning our day out when she woke up. After we ate, we got up and got dressed. Then, I heard her scream. I ran to the bedroom to find her on the floor with water all around her, so I cleaned her up and called her mom to let her know I was taking her to the hospital.

We had to make it to Columbus because she didn't want to go to a nearby hospital. I headed down 103 with my foot to the floor. Every bridge and bump we hit, she screamed at me and gave me that 'I will whip your ass if you do that again' look. We made it to the hospital, and her mom and aunt were standing at the emergency room door waiting on our arrival. The nurse came out to meet us and rolled her in as I parked the car. Whitney was already dilated to seven centimeters, and our baby girl wasn't waiting. By the time her doctor arrived, she was already in push mode.

Ten minutes later, we had a beautiful seven-pound eight-ounce baby girl. I had to be the first to hold her. When I looked into her eyes, it was like she was begging me to keep her and never let her go, but her mom had already made that decision for us. Tears rolled down my face as I told my beautiful little angel that I loved her. As I handed her back to the nurse, I had to step out of the room for a moment to gather my thoughts and calm down before I said something I might regret later.

As I waited in the hallway, Mekia called and asked me if I could come down for the weekend. I told her, "I don't know, baby. I will let you know later on in the week, okay?"

She replied, "Okay. That's fine, so what are you doing, Monta?"

"Just handling some business at the moment, but I will call you later." I took a deep breath, walked back in the room, and held Whitney's hand. She was lying there crying. It bothered me to see the hurt in her face over a decision she made, but I made her a promise that I would be by her side, and that promise I couldn't break.

The nurse took the baby to the nursery. The thoughts that ran through my head as I watched her aunt follow her made tears fall even more. All that I could do was comfort Whitney and let her know that it was going to be okay. I didn't even believe that lie myself, but I had to make sure I kept my promise that, no matter what, I would be supportive.

As they rolled Whitney to her room, I strolled behind them, angry as hell. If I acted out, I would upset Whitney, and I didn't want to do that at that point, but the rage was coming. I sat by her side for hours as she cried and cried. "Baby, what did I do? Why couldn't you stop me?" she asked.

Knowing I had neglected her, I tried not to say anything that would be even more painful. I just said that I was sorry for not being everything she needed and just held her hand tighter. Her mom walked in, and behind her was the nurse with our beautiful baby girl. Her eyes were like the eyes I fell in love with; she looked just like her mom. I picked her up and handed her to Whitney's mom, and they played.

The smile that our bundle of joy gave Whitney was a smile of peace and love, the way that the storybooks speak of. To see their bond and know it was going to be cut short just did something to my soul. As they closed their tired eyes, I sat and stared at the beauty that we created together. Even though I loved Whitney deeply, I still loved Precious more. I didn't know how many hearts I'd broken trying to find Precious in someone, which would never happen. All that I could do was hope and pray that, one day, she would find herself back in my arms. Since it was getting late, I had to get back up the road. I kissed Whitney and my daughter goodnight and headed to the house.

Shevonne called and asked, "What are you doing?"

"On my way home. What's up?"

"Nothing. Just trying to see what you doing. How long will it take before you get to the house?" she asked.

"Not that long. I will probably be there in fifteen minutes."

"Okay. I'll be waiting on you," she said.

The closer I got to the house, the more my mind wandered. The last time she came over, she ran my company off, so what would it be this time? I pulled up, and she was sitting in her car. We both got out, went into the house, and started something I thought would never happen again. From the living room to the bedroom, the heat was smoking, and we were dancing to the music we made ten years back that still sounded the same. I don't know what came over us. All I know is it came, and so did I.

Shevonne stayed the night, but all I could do was think about my baby and how long it would be before they took her away. The next morning, we woke up to the birds outside my window. We got dressed, and Shevonne went her way, and I went mine. I looked down at my phone and saw that it had been very busy during the night with calls from Whitney and Mekia. I had to call and check on my baby first to see how she was doing and ask if they needed anything.

"Hey, beautiful. How are you?" I asked.

"I'm fine, just tired. She took all my energy, and I'm hungry. Will you bring me something to eat, please?" Whitney asked.

"Yes, I can do that. What do you want?"

"You can go by KFC and get me something and get me a sweet tea."

"I will be there in an hour, baby. I love you guys!"

"And we love you too, handsome. See you when you get here."

"Okay, baby. Kiss my baby for me."

"The nurse just came in and got her, but I will when she comes back."

"Whitney, I just want to say that I really love you. I know this process is hard, but I'm here for you, sweetheart. I will help you through this, okay."

"Thank you so much, Monta! You don't know how much it means to hear you say that."

"I just want what's best for you and our baby. Even though it's not right to me, I got you, baby." I continued to talk to Whitney as I pulled into KFC and placed her order. Then, I drove to the hospital and got out, juggling a bag and soda in my hands. "I'm downstairs. I will see you when I get there. I'm getting into the elevator," I told Whitney as I stepped on the elevator and stared into the eyes of this little five foot three angel with beautiful gray eyes and an awesome smile. "Hey, how are you?" I asked.

"I'm fine, and yourself?"

"I'm wonderful now since you're about to give me your phone number," I said to the angel.

"And who said I was?"

"I did. I'm Monta, by the way."

"Hey, Monta, I'm Crystal."

"So, Crystal, are you taken?"

"No, I'm not. What about you?"

"Well, I am now."

"You going to the third floor? Who are you down here to see?" she asked.

"My baby momma."

"Well, at least you're honest. Here is my number. Call me when you leave here."

"Okay, I will talk to you later."

Walking down the hall, I could hear my angel crying. I stepped into the room where she and her mom were going at it.

"What's wrong with my baby?" I asked Whitney, who was struggling with our daughter's diaper.

"She doesn't want to get her pamper changed!" Whitney said.

"Because, baby, you don't know what you're doing. Look, let me show you." I took over changing the pamper and then picked my little angel up. "See, daddy got Cee Cee all dry."

"Cee Cee! I love that, Monta, so Cee Cee it is."

"When are they going to discharge you?" I asked.

"The doctor said in the morning after he comes in and checks the baby and I. After he checks her, my aunt is taking her home with her." She paused and looked at me before adding, "Monta, I want you here to sign these papers so she can have your last name."

"I will be here, baby. I promise."

"So, what did you do last night when you left without saying anything, punk?" she asked playfully.

"Nothing. I just went to the house, and I didn't want to wake you up, baby. You were sleeping so peacefully. And I got your punk. That's why Cee Cee had you screaming yesterday."

"Really, Monta! That's not funny, at all!"

"Well, it was funny to me. You didn't see me laughing?"

"No. I was in too much pain to see anything. Monta, can I ask you a question?"

"Yes, baby, you can ask me anything you want."

"Was I not good enough for you? I mean, give me a reason why you just walked away from me and went to another woman. I thought we were a perfect couple."

"We were and still are. See, baby, what I did had nothing to do with you. I mean, I couldn't have asked for a better person to have in my life. From the start, you were perfect from your hello to your goodnights. The attention you gave me the first night we met was unbelievable. Hell, you were unbelievable, Whitney."

"Baby, I wish we could go back to that night and just start all over again. Monta, you just don't know how you make me feel. I know your heart is still with Precious, but with time, I can change that."

"Whitney, you are a perfect and beautiful young lady, and you have a lot going for yourself, but someone replacing Precious is unthinkable. I'm not trying to be mean, but I'm real, and the truth I have to speak. I love you, but she has my heart. But you can try; I will give you that. You are the only one worthy of that chance, and that's just being real."

"So, Monta, where do we go from here?"

"Well, you know it would have been a lot easier if you wouldn't have given up our daughter. We would have that building bond with her and the connection that we all would have experienced. It's done now, so all we can do is hope and pray that this doesn't come between us."

"Well, I'm not going to let it. I pray that you don't, Monta."

"I love you, Whitney. I will be here in the morning so we can sign her papers," I said as I got ready to leave.

"Why are you leaving, Monta? You're not staying the night with us?"

"Baby, I have to go home and shower."

"Yeah, I know you don't like to be nasty. Well, we love you, handsome, and please be on time in the morning."

"I will, baby. I promise."

Chapter Eleven

"Hey, beautiful, so we meet again. I see you must want me bad, huh?" I said after running into Crystal on the way to my car.

"Maybe or maybe not. Let's go see!" she said, sounding bold.

"Where are we going?"

"Wherever you take me. Just handle me with care," Crystal said.

"Oh, trust me, I will."

"So, Monta, tell me about you. Who are you, and what do you like to do?"

"Well, I'm a gentleman, so ladies first."

"Okay. I like that. As you know, my name is Crystal. I'm twenty-four with no kids. I'm a senior at Columbus State. I don't drink nor smoke, and I hate clubs, I love to shop and just enjoy life. My dad is a doctor, and my mom is also. I'm going to be a surgeon. That's what I've wanted to do since I was six, and I'm sticking to my dream."

"Well, I'm twenty-seven, and I don't drink or smoke. I have seven kids, and I'm going to school to get my business degree, and like you, I don't club. I love to cook and enjoy life.

I race motorcycles, and as you know, my name is Monta, and I'm fine as hell."

"Yes, you are. I have to give it to you, Monta. You are fine as hell!"

"And so are you, sweetheart. You know I wish I could take you back home with me," I said, putting it out there.

"That would be nice, but I have school in the morning. Plus, if I don't come home, my dad would kill you and me."

"Damn that. He might kill you. On the other hand, with me, that would be a shootout. But I have to be back down here in the morning, so you would be good."

"I don't have any clothes with me, Monta."

"I'll take you to your house so that you can get some clothes."

"I don't know about that, Monta. Just take me back to my car, and I will go home, get some clothes, and just tell them I'm going to stay with my friend in her dorm room. Then, I can get back out and go park my car at the school."

"How far away from the hospital do you stay?" I asked.

"We live in the Hills and Dales Estate about ten minutes away."

I told her, "Okay. I will just wait here for you."

"Nope, you can ride with me. They won't see you, not from where I park my car anyway."

"Well, let me get my pistol out of the car real quick. You can never know what might happen."

"Monta, I promise you that nothing will happen."

We headed to her house, and as we reached the neighborhood, my eyes saw shit that you wouldn't think that Columbus had—houses almost taller than tall buildings. As we approached her house, I just knew I had to get into this family. I had never seen a house with a six-car garage before, and parked out front was a Lamborghini. I could only imagine what was behind the garage doors. A little while after going inside, Crystal ran back out and jumped in the car, smiling. "I told you that they wouldn't see you."

"They might not have seen me, but I bet those cameras did. They were looking right at the car."

"Baby, trust me. You weren't seen," she said with a smile.

"So, you just want to drive your car to my house? I can just leave mine at the hospital if you want to."

"I wanted you to drop me off in front of the building. If I drive, my dad might just ride by and check to see if I'm really here," Crystal said.

"Well, let's go get my car then. I don't want to get your grown-ass in any trouble."

"Really, Monta, it's not like that. I just try to respect my parents while I'm in their house."

"And that you should. So, why are you going to my house? I mean, isn't that being disrespectful?"

"Monta, I'm twenty-four years old and never even kissed a guy because I was kept in the house under guard twenty-four/seven. I just can't take it anymore. I have toys, but I want to feel something real, and you just had to bump into me."

"Oh, wow! I don't think you want me to be your first, sweetheart."

Crystal had a serious look on her face when she said, "And why not? We don't have to have any ties. I just want to know what it would feel like to be with a man."

"So, you're saying if you would have met someone else, then it would still be the same outcome?" I asked as I tried to feel her out. Her story about never kissing a man didn't go along with her ditching her car to go back to my place for the night, especially since we just met.

"No, I'm not a hoe if that's what you are trying to say!"

"No, sweetheart. That's not what I'm saying. Look, don't worry about it. Just go park your car, and I will follow you." We headed to the school with my mind wandering. If she was twenty-four and easy for me to get her attention so quickly, then who else's bite was so vicious?

We pulled up to the campus, and she parked her car and got in with me. Our conversation was straight to the point as we headed up the road. I wanted to know more about her background and her motive. I just had bought some cucumbers the day before, so I already had my plan working in my mind.

I took shortcuts through West Point to throw off her path and vision of things to look for to get back. We pulled up to the house, and I opened her door. She smiled and said, "Thanks."

We entered the house, sat down, and talked for a while. Then, she got up and showered. My mind was still roaming, but it was time to go into beast mode. I was thinking, if she really was a virgin, I would have to be careful with her. She stepped out the shower and into the hallway stark naked. Her body was perfect, not a mark on it as she looked at me all shy and innocently.

I walked up to her and kissed her on the cheek, and she blushed. I picked her up, carried her to the bedroom, and laid her down so gently on my bed. She pulled me up and started kissing me. At that point, I could tell that this was her first time kissing, so I stuck my finger in her mouth, got it wet, and kissed down her neck as I slid my finger in her pussy. Right off, I knew she was a virgin, so it was playtime.

I put my playlist on and went to work, taking my time with her. I taught her how to kiss, where to kiss, and the passion kissing brings. I made my way down to her breasts, and she moaned so, so sexily. I made my way to the valley, and like a stream of water on a sunny day, the sight was so beautiful. I placed her legs on my shoulders and kissed her lips. Then, I licked her clit, and she moaned even louder. I started sucking on her clit, and she went wild, so I slid my finger in her pussy and got it wet, stroking her so slowly. I slid my other finger in her ass, and she came so strong and so long. Still taking my time, I put another finger in her pussy. She jumped, letting me know it was too much. I calmed her down by coaching her through the pain and process.

H-Town "Knocking the Boots" came on, and my mind went left. I put her on my shoulders and went to work. Her legs started shaking, and she got scared when she started squirting and lost her mind. I laid her down, slid my head in, and stroked her slowly. As I went further and further inside, her nails went deeper and deeper into my skin. Tears fell, and my back bled.

She said, "It hurts, Monta!"

I wasn't trying to hook her because I didn't need any more of those problems. The session got more intense after I told her, "If you take my pain, I will take yours."

She looked in my eyes and said, "Please, Monta, don't leave me!"

At that moment, I knew I had messed up, so I didn't care anymore. I went deeper, and her cries got louder. She came even more, and her nails went deeper into my skin. I stroked slower and harder, knowing I had her just where I needed her. It was time to send her to space. I grinded so smooth with the slowest thrusts ever as I watched her eyes roll into the back of her head. I could see her soul leaving her body. Knowing she would go alone, I just kept doing my art. The only woman I painted with and lost myself into was Precious, and I prayed for that hit again daily.

I turned Crystal over, arched her back, and went in from the back. She fell down, holding her stomach, ending our session. I picked her up, took her into the shower, and cleaned her up. Then, I showered, and we got dressed. I cooked her dinner, and we laid it down. Lying next to her nakedness as we talked got me all hot and bothered again. I started stroking my dick, and she said, "Let's do it again."

Knowing we had an early morning, we did a quick session and went to sleep. The next morning, my phone went off, and we jumped up and got in the shower. Watching the water run down Crystal's body turned me on. I couldn't resist it, so I bent her over and slid it in, stroking her as the water hit the back of her ass, bouncing off and hitting me in my chest and face. As the strokes got harder, she looked back at me and said, "Baby, I'm about to come."

At that moment, I had to go deep so that I could climax with her. We both reached that point, and I couldn't pull out. That pussy was so good, wet, and tight it had my dick in a chokehold. We got out of the shower, got dressed, and headed down the road, talking and laughing about last night. She said she enjoyed her session and that she wanted to do it again later on tonight.

She asked me if I could be her man. Not wanting to break her heart, I just said, "Let's see how this goes." I didn't want to get tied up with anyone else, but I would entertain her for a while.

We pulled up to her building, and she kissed me and jumped out of the car, running to her class. As soon as I pulled out the school's parking lot, Whitney called to ask where I was located.

"I'm in Columbus, baby," I told her.

"Well, come on because they will be around for you to sign the papers in a minute. The doctor already came by to check the baby and me," Whitney said.

"I will be there in five minutes, baby. How are you feeling?" I asked.

"I don't want to give my baby up!"

"I know, baby, but you signed a legally binding agreement."

"I know, and that's what hurts. I didn't know if you would be a part of our life, and I had already signed the deal with the record label. There wasn't much I could do with a baby on my hip. I did what I thought would be the best for both of us, but now I know that it wasn't. Monta, my heart is hurting so bad that I cried all night long. I haven't even been to sleep. The nurse came in here and sat with me for three hours. We talked a lot, but I couldn't stop the tears from falling."

"Well, I'm here now, baby. You don't have to cry anymore. We will fix it, okay?"

"You always know what to say to make me feel better, Monta."

"That's what I'm here for, baby. Whitney, I love you with everything in me, and don't you ever forget that."

"Can I come home with you, Monta?"

"Don't you have to go with your aunt tomorrow to take the baby to the doctor?" I asked.

"I don't know. Let me ask the doctor," Whitney said, and I could hear her conversation with a female nurse. "Excuse me. Is Dr. Henderson still here?" she asked.

"Yes, he is next door. Do you need to see him?" the nurse replied.

"Yes, could you please tell him to come to see me. I have a question for him," Whitney said.

"Is it anything that I could help you with?" the nurse asked.

"I don't know. I just needed to know if I would have to go with my aunt to take the baby to the doctor tomorrow?" Whitney asked.

"You signed your rights to her, right?"

"Yes, ma'am, I did."

"Yes, the first two visits, you would have to go with her."

"Oh, okay. Thank you. That's all I wanted to know, and again thank you."

As soon as Whitney finished talking to the nurse, I said, "Baby, I will spend the day with you guys and take care of you both until your aunt picks her up."

"Thank you so much, baby. That's why I love you so much, Monta. You are the best! Cee Cee and I have the best man in this world. When I record my first single, I want you right by my side. I wouldn't have it any other way."

"Baby, I will be right there, cheering you on with my sign and balloons."

"Really, baby? Balloons? Now you're trying to embarrass us. You hear your dad, Cee Cee? This man talking about having a sign and balloons at the studio! Now, what do you think about that, princess?"

"She said her daddy can do whatever he wants. Isn't that right, princess?" I asked and cooed at my beautiful daughter.

"Monta, what are we going to do? I want this every day. We are a family now, and a happy one at that, and I ruined it."

"No, you didn't, sweetheart. I told you I will fix it, so don't worry about it. If I tell you I got something, just count it done already, okay sexy?"

"Okay, handsome. See, you got me all horny up in this hospital, and I'm all bleeding and shit. They talking about I have to wait six weeks before I can have any sexual intercourse."

"Well, you do, baby. We can do it as soon as you stop bleeding."

"And how long does that take?"

"Depends on your body. We will handle that when that time comes."

"Okay then, but you know that I'm addicted to you, Monta. Six weeks is a long ass time to be off my meds."

"Girl, you crazy, but I feel you, though. I will buy you a toy so you can play Bloody Mary at night."

"Really? So you being funny now, huh?"

"No, baby, I'm sorry," I said and laughed at Whitney as she pouted.

***

"Well, now that you guys got all the papers signed, you can leave. Let me get you a chair, so I can roll you and the baby down," the nurse said to Whitney and then turned to me. "Dad, you go bring the car around, and we will meet you at the front."

I went and pulled the car around, picked my ladies up, and headed to the house. "Baby, do you want me to stop and get you something to eat?"

"Yes, please. You can go by Zaxby's and get me something, baby."

"You sure? I can call Long Horn or Applebee's, baby."

"That does sound good, Monta. Order me a steak and some fries and steamed vegetables. Do you want anything to eat, baby?"

"No, I'm not hungry, sweetheart. I just want to make sure that you're okay."

"Thank you for being my superman, Monta. I would have never thought of meeting someone like you. You have a heart of gold and always thinking of others, and you love me. The way you love me is amazing. The way you kiss me is wow so amazing! You touch my soul with every kiss! Shit, let me stop talking about it because it's making me horny."

"Baby, you have me forever, so you have time."

"Monta, I wish we could just go home with you tonight. I want to lay in your arms and just snuggle up with you."

"I wish you could, baby. That would really be awesome."

"Yes, it would, so what do you want to do today, baby?"

"You can't do anything, Whitney. You have to rest. You can write some songs and sing them to me. That would be great. You have to remember the harder you work, the better you are going to be, and we have nothing but time. Just write until you get tired, and make sure they are slow songs. You know I love them slow jams. I mean, if you want me to buy one."

"Really, Monta? You know you don't have to buy my music when you have the vocals right here with you."

"I know, baby, but I can't play you through my radio."

"Boy, you're crazy, but that's what I love about you. You know how to make me smile. I already know that she is going to be just like you."

"Hold on, baby. My brother is calling," I told Whitney as I answered Truck's call. "What's up, cat daddy?"

"Where you at, boy?" he asked.

"I'm in Columbus. What you got going on?"

"Those boys got a new bike and want to race you," he said, and I could hear the sound of money in his voice.

I asked, "How much are they trying to bet?"

"They said it don't matter. Bet what you want to bet!"

"Okay, I'm on my way, and tell them we don't have time for all that talking and shit." I ended the call with Truck and told Whitney, "Baby, I will be back. Let me go make this money for you."

"Okay, baby. Be careful, and hurry back! Monta, I'm not playing with you now. You better hurry back," she said with a serious look on her face.

"I love you two!" I said as I walked toward the door.

"And we love you, too, handsome!" Whitney said, smiling. I was glad she was in good spirits and happy.

As I headed out the door, Crystal called to say she was ready and already had her clothes. I swung by the school to pick her up and headed to West Point.

"Hey, handsome, how has your day been?" she asked when she got in the car.

"It's been great. Picked up my baby momma and my baby. How has your day been?" I asked her.

"It's been wonderful! I was walking to my class and felt something running out of me. I went to the bathroom, and I saw something bloody," she said, and I knew she had no idea of what was happening with her body.

"That's normal, baby. You just lost your virginity, and as we call it, you got your cherry popped!" I told her.

"Well, it had me scared. I didn't know what to do. I saw my friend and got a pad from her, but we're good now, baby."

We made it to my brother's house, and the street was packed. He had already pulled the bike out, so I got out of the car and was already on go. We got the money up and headed to the back road. Crystal jumped in the truck with my brother, and we got to the spot and picked our lanes. After waiting on the flagman to get set, he motioned for us to start the burnouts. I finished my burnout and pulled up to the line. My competition pulled up and gave his signal, and I just sat back and gave mine.

The flagman dropped his hand, and that was the last I saw of him. I crossed the finish line when my competition was just halfway down the stretch. He made it across the line and said he wanted to run it back double or nothing, so I agreed. We pulled back up to the starting line. I dry-hopped and lined up. My competition pulled up and signaled. I signaled, and he dropped his hand. I let that boy take off while I sat there until my brother said, "Go!"

When I twisted the throttle, she took off. When I went to second gear, I was two bikes ahead. All I could do was shake my head on that nice payday. I turned around and didn't even stop. I went back to my brother's house, pulled the bike back in the garage, and waited on them to pull up. Truck and my girl were the first to pull up. They jumped out the car laughing, saying I shouldn't have did him like that. But hell, he came for that, and I gave it to him just like he liked it, straight across his ass.

We hung out for a while. Then, we went and got a bite to eat and headed to the house. Once home, we jumped in the shower, and it went down—hair pulling, back-scratching, hot, steamy sex from the tub to the bed, from the bed to the couch, and the script ended there. We sat on the couch stark naked, eating and laughing.

The night went a little longer than I planned. I had a long trip in the morning, heading to spend the weekend with Mekia, so we laid down. I tossed and turned until the sun came up, but Crystal slept like a newborn. We got up, dressed, and headed to Columbus.

I dropped Crystal off at the school and stopped by to see Whitney and my baby for a while then took off towards

Blakely. I had a two-hour drive on a long, lonely road after a night with no sleep. I made it to Mekia's house, and she wanted to talk, but I needed sleep. She wanted to make music, and all that I could say was, "Baby, can I get a short nap in? I been up all night long."

Mekia said, "Well, I have to run to the store to get something to cook, so you need to go on and get that nap out the way. When I get back, I'm going to need you deep off in my guts. I have waited a long time for this."

"Well, when you get back, I will be ready," I said and drifted off to sleep.

Mekia took her time, and that was okay with me. I woke up around six that night, and I was in the house alone. I went into the kitchen, made dinner, and watched TV until she and her boys came home.

"Baby, you up now, I see. We came home, and you were knocked out, so I just took the boys to their baseball game."

"I told you that I was tired, baby. It took everything in me to keep my eyes open coming here, but now that I'm up and rested, you know what it is! Let's feed the kids, so you can feed me." We looked into each other's eyes for a while, and I knew that she knew what would come next.

"Oh, so you hungry, huh?" she asked, teasingly.

I replied, "I can eat only if you're serving."

We got the boys fed and settled. Then, we showered and got into bed. For some reason, I just wasn't turned on by her anymore. No matter what I did, I couldn't light the fire in me, so I pleased her and called it a night.

The next day, I was ready to go home, but I stayed to give it another chance. We hung out all day, went to her mom's house for a while, and got ready for bed. Again, the same outcome. Being who I am, I told her, "It's nothing about you that turns me on." Then, I went to sleep without even seeing how she would respond to my admission.

On my way back home the next day, I stopped by and checked on Whitney and the baby.

"Monta, did you really not talk to me all weekend? I tried calling you and kept getting your voicemail!" Whitney said, sounding upset.

"Baby, I'm sorry. I told you that I was going out of town on some business," I explained.

"But you know my aunt will be getting Cee Cee tomorrow!" she fussed.

"So, what do you want to do today?" I asked, changing the subject.

"Let me get her dressed. I will get some clothes on, and we can go up the road," Whitney said.

"You want to go to West Point?"

"No, crazy! I'm talking about Atlanta. I want to buy her some things to take with her and to get you whatever you want," she said.

"I don't want anything. As long as I have you two, I don't need anything else. We are about to enjoy this day with our princess and celebrate your signing! That is a great accomplishment, and I'm so proud of you, and I love you more than you would ever know, but I have to be honest with you. I've been seeing someone else. I mean, I have a problem. I just can't have one woman. It's not satisfying to me," I admitted.

"Monta, you just don't get it, do you? As long as I'm your main, I don't give a damn about no other woman. If it's not Precious, I'm not worried. She is the only threat for now."

"Whitney, why do you love me so much? I mean, what is it about me that grabs your attention?"

"Well, Monta, you are the kindest person I know. You love me for me, and you have always treated me with respect. Since that night we met, you have been nothing but great to me and my family. You only wanted what was best for me and made sure that it was granted."

"Whitney, it's hard to find an honest woman. In today's time, women don't know if they want to be a girl or boy. Ninety percent of them are mad for no reason and want to cry about how they can't find a good man. Hell, they ran all of them off with that crying and bitching. You were different. Your approach was different. You didn't come at me with your hand out begging. That's why anything you ever wanted I made sure you had."

She replied, "And that you did, and I thank you for showing me what real love is like."

I drove Whitney to Atlanta, and that day was one of the best days we had together. She shopped, we ate, and we laughed. Whitney wasn't Precious, but she would make a man's heart melt. We headed back down the road. She wanted to stay with me but had to be home by eight in the morning. We couldn't chance that, so I just stayed the night with her. She laid in my arms, and I held her so tight to let her know everything was okay. I didn't want that night to end. For once in a long time, I turned my phone off so we could have peace without anyone disturbing our last night with our princess.

Morning shined through the window, letting us know it was time to get up and get dressed. Whitney packed all of Cee Cee's things, and as she was finishing up, she broke down. "What did I do? How could I let this happen?" she cried out as her tears fell.

We had to be at the office by eight, so I just finished packing the bags and loaded the car. There wasn't much I could say to change how she felt. I just grabbed her hand and held it tight.

That day was a hard day for us. It did something to our relationship. For the rest of the day, we hardly spoke and couldn't stand being next to each other. Even though she loved me, and I loved her, things weren't the same anymore between us.

Chapter Twelve

As time passed on, Crystal and I were still going strong. Turned out, she was pregnant with my son. Her parents didn't like the fact that I got their daughter pregnant, but I told Crystal I would always be there for her and our child. Then, one day, I got a call from my ex-wife Shevonne with the news that she was pregnant also. That was a surprise and shifted everything in my life, but I told her the same thing as I told Crystal. I would be there for my child.

Meanwhile, I had a new friend I was getting close to. Me and a girl named Marion started kicking it and talking on the phone every day. One sunny day in May, as I was leaving work, my phone rang. The number looked familiar, but I couldn't believe I was seeing this number on my phone screen after all this time. I answered the phone to a crying, hurt young lady. Not knowing what to say, I asked, "What's wrong, Miya? Why are you crying?"

"He left me!" was all she said.

"Who left you? And if he left you then it's his loss, not yours. Don't ever allow a man to see you sweat, Miya. At the end of the day, if he just up and leaves, then he was never there."

We talked until she calmed down. She thanked me for listening to her cries, and we said our goodnights. We talked for the next few weeks off and on, but Marion and I spoke every day. Marion and I made plans to go out one weekend in June. She and her son came down, and we hung out, went to the beach, and back to the room. We watched TV until her son fell asleep, and then she jumped in the shower, and I jumped in right behind her.

When I got out, she was standing there all sexy, looking tasty and all. I put on one of my favorite playlists, and magic began to take place. She climbed on the bed and posed as if she knew I was about to fuck her head up. I put on my wet suit because I was about to make a thunderstorm in those sheets.

I kissed her lips softly as she melted into the bed, and I traveled down her body. Through her mountains, I roamed on down to her valley. I embedded my tongue, sucking on her clit and stroking her pussy as she creamed and moaned. Trying not to wake her son, she buried her face in the pillows. As I put on a show, she came and came.

Pulling me up, she grabbed my dick and put it in her tight pussy, not knowing what she was getting herself into. She couldn't scream through the pain. With every stroke, tears rolled down her face. She pulled me close, begging me to cum. She squirted and squirted, scratching my back as I flipped her on her side. I went deeper and deeper as she bit the pillow. With her eyes closed tightly, body shaking, and her nails deep in my flesh, she whispered so softly, "Please, please cum, Monta."

My session wasn't finished, so I stood up, lifted her weak body off the bed, and dropped dick down in her tight pussy, stretching her walls. Tears started to fall more and more. With no control of her body, she couldn't do anything but take what she'd been asking for over the past months. I lowered her body down, slowed my strokes, and went into grind mode, slowly grinding her pussy, sucking on her nipples. She forgot about her pain and began to lose herself in the zone. Her moaning grew more and more intense, and my grind got deeper and deeper.

I whispered in her ear, "Do you feel daddy's dick?"

"Yes, daddy. I feel your big dick!"

"Do you love daddy's dick?"

"Yessssssssss, daddy. I'm about to cum on daddy's dick."

Knowing exactly what I was doing, I went into finishing mode. I pulled my dick out and pushed it in with a hard stroke. I let go, filling her up with all the stress I had in me.

Afterward, she laid in my arms, and we talked until we fell asleep. The next morning around five, I woke up and showered. Then, I woke her up, and she took her shower. We laid in bed, talking about a possible future. Precious still had my heart, so it was hard to completely give myself to another woman. It wasn't fair to the hearts I crossed, but I was trying to find what I was missing in someone else instead of going to the person who I had lost myself in.

Before they headed home, we got dressed and went to breakfast. Then, we said our goodbyes. My brother called and told me to get my ass down the road so we could load up and go to the track. I headed to his house, and we loaded the bikes up and went to the track. It was nice and pretty out, and the track was packed with bikes everywhere. I just knew we were going to have a great day. I had a pocket full of money and three bottles full of nitrous, so anybody could get it. We didn't care who it was. If they lined up beside either one of our bikes, we were going across their ass.

Our first race was Pumpkin Head. He had a big motorbike, but we didn't give a damn today. We lined up, and when those lights dropped, I cut the tree down on him. I could hear that big motor coming, but he wasn't coming fast enough. We pulled back around to the ticket booth, and he wanted to do it again. We went back to the starting line and let the bikes cool down before we got back on the track. My brother pushed me in the water box, and I did my burn, and he did his. Pumpkin Head staged, then I rolled in my beams and turned my second bulb on.

As Pumpkin Head rolled into his beam, the light dropped. I cut the tree down again, but when that gas hit, it picked the front tire up, and we crossed the finish line first on one wheel. As the night came to an end, Doctor Cool called us out on one of the cleanest and fastest 1000s around. Everybody was betting with Cool, so we got the money up, switched out the nitrous bottle, and headed to the staging lanes.

For once, I was on pins and needles, and so was he. Everybody knew Taz didn't play any games, and we knew that 1000s were quick and fast. We pushed the bikes in the water box, shook hands, and got on the bikes. He started his bike, and I started Taz. We did our burnouts and rolled in the first beam at the same time. I looked at him, and he looked back at me. He rolled in, and as I was rolling, the light dropped.

At the same time, we left the light like a rocket. I could hear that 1000 waking up, but Taz wasn't hearing that noise. I pulled him half a bike as we went down the track. I could still hear that 1000, but knowing I was out front, I looked back at him as I crossed the finish line. I could feel the pressure let off of my chest. I stopped on the return road to take a breath because I just knew that race was going to go down to the wire.

Cool stopped, shook my hand, and said, "Good race! I knew that if anybody was going to beat me today it was going to be you. You're one of the best riders I have ever seen, and I race all over."

"Good race, Cool," I told him and headed back up the return road.

I could see my crew coming towards me, happy and cheering. I stopped at the trailer and parked the bike to let it cool off. Taz had showed out enough for one day.

As we walked back up to the starting line, a young lady looked at me and said, "That damn Taz is kicking up dust again!" All that I could do was look at her and smile.

Truck said, "Bro, you rode the hell out of Taz then!"

We hung out at the start line, tripping, betting, and making money until it was time to go. Then, we loaded the bikes up, headed to Truck's house, and dropped the trailer. After a very good day, I headed home. As I was pulling into the yard, Miya called.

"What are you doing?" she asked.

"Nothing much. Just leaving the track," I told her.

She asked, "What is that?"

"A racetrack. I race motorcycles."

"Oh, okay. I bet that's fun."

"It is. You need to come see me one weekend."

"Can I see you tomorrow?" she asked.

"Yeah, we can make that happen. When I get off tomorrow, I will come home, shower, and head your way." I finished making plans to visit Miya and hung up, went into the house, and got ready for bed.

As I was laying down, my phone rung. It was Crystal, so I answered it.

"Hey, Monta, what you doing?"

"Nothing. Getting in bed. What you up to?"

"Nothing much. Just missing you, that's all!"

"Oh, really? I thought your parents told you not to speak to me anymore."

"I know, and that hurt me so bad. I called to let you know they are sending me to Texas with my uncle. I'm not supposed to be calling you, but I want you to be there when I have our son," she said. I could hear the sadness in her voice.

"Well, sweetheart, all you have to do is call me, and I will be there."

Her voice cracked even more as she told me, "That's the thing. I won't be able to call you."

"Then, how am I going to know, Crystal?" I asked.

"Why don't you just come and get me. I don't want to go. I don't want to be away from you. These past months have been killing me, not seeing nor talking to you. They took my phone and car, and they were taking me to school. They were telling me I was a disgrace to our family's name and that I should be whipped. That's when I drew the line. They are not going to touch me! I told them, if they put their hands on me, I was going to call you to come and get me."

"Look, Crystal, if you want me to, I will come get you now. I mean, you're a grown-ass woman. You don't have to do shit they say, really."

"I know, but I try to be respectful to my parents."

"And you're supposed to be, but you're not a child anymore. You're saying that they are sending you off like you're a ten-year-old. Look, you and my child can come stay with me."

"That's what I want to do, but they are not going to let me leave out of the house. I leave tomorrow, so it would be difficult."

"How would it be difficult, baby? I pull up, and you get your shit and get in the car with me. I mean, it's that simple."

"No, baby. My dad wouldn't go for that."

"You must not know who I am, Crystal?"

"Baby, I just don't want to cause any problems."

"You won't be causing any problems, Crystal. I will be the one causing the problems."

"Monta, let me call you back, okay? I love you!" she said and hung up.

I laid in bed for a minute just thinking before I closed my eyes. The next morning, I awakened to my alarm clock and got dressed for work. As I headed out the door, my phone rang. On the other end was a weeping voice saying, "Hello..."

I didn't recognize the number, but the voice I knew so, so well.

"Good morning, Whitney. How you doing?"

"Not so good," she said, sniffling.

"What's wrong?"

"Monta, I miss you, and I can't get you or our daughter out of my head. I want you, Monta, and I need you in my life."

"Well, Whitney, you made your choice, and all I could do was respect it. On the other hand, I heard your single, and I'm super proud of you and all that you have accomplished."

"Monta, it doesn't mean anything when you are without your family. I threw you and our daughter away. This money and fame don't mean shit to me without you guys here with me."

"Well, I'm seeing someone else now, sweetheart."

"But what about me, Monta? What am I supposed to do? You're the reason I'm here, and I told you when I go to the top I want you here beside me."

"I will talk to you later, Whitney. Or you could just text me, okay? I love you."

"Well, if you love me, take me back, Monta. Please!"

"Sweetheart, we had our time, and it didn't work. We need to just move on with our lives and just be friends," I told her.

"I don't want to be your damn friend, Monta. Why are you doing this to me?" Whitney yelled.

"Like I said, text me. Talk to you later, Whitney."

After talking to Whitney, my whole day was messed up. I couldn't think straight. My mind was running in six different directions. My heart wanted to be with her, but my mind wanted different. All I could think about was our last time together and all the memories we shared.

Miya helped take my mind off Whitney throughout the day. We texted off and on, talking about our meeting later that night. As 5:00 rolled around, I cleaned up the shop and headed to the house to get showered and dressed.

As I walked out the door, Truck called and said we had a race set up for the weekend, so I stopped by his house and got all the info on what our plans were and who we had to race. I left his house, heading to Columbus. Riding down this road brought back memories. I remembered this drive when I was going to see the mother of my daughter, the closest thing I would ever get to Precious. Now, she's a past love too, but my heart still held her close.

I pulled up to the place where me and Miya were meeting, and as I pulled into the parking spot, she bent the corner. We greeted each other with a hug.

"Hey, Monta! How was your day?" she asked.

"It was great, and yours?"

"Well, it could have been better. The calls at work were horrible!"

"I'm sorry to hear that," I answered as we were strolling down the river walk catching up.

Her voice was so soft and sweet to my ears that I got caught up in the motion of her lips as if it was our first time meeting. We sat down on the bench and watched the flow of the current as we talked. The conversation was so deep that we lost track of time.

It was time to say our goodnights, but I got caught up in her eyes as we stared at each other. I leaned in, and her lips met mine. She fell into my arms, and the fireworks went off. As I ran my tongue across her bottom lip, I could feel her body get weak. I pulled away because I wasn't trying to get her caught up in the trap that I just let Whitney out of. I walked her to the car, and we said our goodnights.

I headed back to West Point with my mind clouded. My music was flowing the way I liked it. Then, the phone call came through that my son was born at 7 p.m. He was eight pounds and three ounces. I could see his picture, but a picture wouldn't do my heart any good. I couldn't hold or kiss him.

Crystal told me, "Monta, I really wish you were here, baby. I was in this all alone. All that I could do was cry. I cried so much that I stressed the baby. His heart rate started dropping, so that made me cry even more. You just don't understand what I just went through. My aunt and uncle just brought me here and dropped me off. My mom and dad said they didn't want to come and see this bastard child. My uncle told me that he was disappointed, so I will be here alone until it's time for us to leave the hospital."

"So, you mean to tell me they took you there and left you, Crystal? What was the purpose of them sending you there if you were going to be treated like shit anyway?" I asked.

"I just want to come home. I don't want to be here!" She sounded so hurt and alone that I felt I had to do something to change that for her.

"Just say the word, and I will come get you. All you have to say is come get me, and I'm there. So do I need to come?" I asked and waited for her to reply. "Crystal, you're not going to answer me?" When she didn't say anything, I told her, "Well, okay. I get it, sweetheart. I'm not trying to stress you, baby. I'm going to let you get some rest. I love you."

"You're just going to leave me alone too, Monta?" she asked as she wept.

"Look, I told you before you left that you could come stay with me. now I'm trying to come get you, and you won't answer me."

"I don't want to make my parents mad," she said softly.

"Man, fuck your parents! They don't give two shits about you, Crystal. I mean, look at your situation. You just had a baby alone with no one there to support you, and you think that's love or concern? I love you, and I want what's best for you and our son. Being there, I don't see that happening. But if you decide to stay, I promise you that you will have all of my help and support that I can give you from here."

"I love you, Monta. You are the best," she said.

We ended the call, and I was thinking about Crystal and my son as I got off 103. Miya called and interrupted my thoughts. We talked until I got home.

"Monta, do you want to spend the weekend together?" she asked.

"I would love that. What you want to do?"

"We could go to the aquarium," Miya suggested.

"That sounds fun. I will come Friday night when I get off work."

"Okay, well, I will be looking forward to this weekend," she said.

"Hey, Miya, make sure you're ready for me because I'm grown as hell."

"I'm always ready. You better be ready," she teased.

"Okay, goodnight, beautiful."

The rest of the week flew by in a hurry. I woke up Friday morning happy and still tired from that night before when I hung out with a longtime friend who didn't want to go home. I got dressed, and my usual morning texts came through, but this time from someone who I had been hoping and praying for, for the last two years.

Precious: Good morning, Monta!

Me: Good morning beautiful. How are you?

Precious: I'm fine, and yourself?

Me: I'm great now that you reached out! I mean this is the text I have been waiting two years for. Every time my phone goes off I wish that it's you. But this morning my prayers were answered.

Precious: So, Monta, what you got going on this morning?

Me: Headed to work baby. What's up?

Precious: I just thought we could just go to breakfast and talk.

Me: Damn I wish this could have been a Saturday. I would love to take you to breakfast, my love, but I have to go to work. Wish I could. Do you think we could do this another time?

Precious: We will see! I have to go back to school.

After that text exchange, I made it to work, and my day went by fast and smooth. I hit the clock as soon as it struck 5:00. I headed to the house, showered, and got ready for my weekend. I met up with Miya, and we got a suite, caught a movie, and grabbed a bite to eat. Then, we headed back to the room.

The next morning, we got up, got dressed, and planned our day out. We ate breakfast and headed to Atlanta. Our drive was great. We had a great conversation. She laughed, and I joked the entire way. Our chemistry was everything that it was supposed to be. We made it to the aquarium with a little time to spare, so we sat in the car and finished our conversation.

"Let's go get the tickets, sweetheart. We have ten minutes until the next showing," I said, and we went to get the tickets.

As we headed over to have a seat, I looked up and saw Bin Laden and about thirty of his guards. Although Miya said it wasn't him, I knew it was. Who else would have thirty people guarding him?

When it was our group's time to go in, I walked through the aquarium with this beautiful young lady on my arm. The feeling was so amazing that I couldn't enjoy the fish. My eyes were glued to her. She walked through, taking pictures, and enjoying the scene. We talked and set our future in stone as we made our way through the aquarium. We stopped by the souvenir shop before we headed out, trying to find something we could always look back on to remind us of this great day.

When we were about to leave, Miya said, "Monta, let's get something to eat."

"Okay. That sounds great. What would you like to eat?" I asked her.

She suggested we go to the Cheesecake Factory, so we left the aquarium, heading towards Cumberland Mall. Walking through the mall, I learned more about what she liked and didn't like. We checked out a few stores and really worked up an appetite, so we worked our way toward the restaurant. As we walked into the restaurant, I saw a familiar face.

"What's up, Monta? What you doing in my part of town?" my cousin Kendell asked.

"Nothing much, cuz. Just came to grab a bite to eat. What you been up to?" I asked.

"Just working, that's all."

"Well, I will catch you later on then," I said.

Me and Miya enjoyed our meal and conversation, got our to-go bag and a slice of cheesecake, and headed out the door. Holding hands as we walked to the car, I opened the door and allowed her to step in and be seated. Her eyes followed my steps as I made my way to the driver's side.

We headed back down the road, talking about our day and the fun we had. As we got off our exit, I stopped by the store to get something to drink. Then, we made it to the suite and settled in. Miya showered, and I followed her. Then, we rested in bed, talking, until she turned over and closed her eyes. In my head, I was thinking this was not supposed to end like this. I got up, put my clothes on, and went downstairs to get some air. When I stepped off the elevator, my eyes landed on this beautiful freckle-faced angel. She smiled at me, and I smiled back.

"Hey, beautiful, how are you?" I asked her.

"I'm fine, and yourself?"

"Well, I will be okay once I get some air."

"What's wrong? Sit down and talk to me," she urged, and something about her made me feel comfortable opening up to her.

"Well, me and this young lady hung out all day. We got back to the room, showered, and got in bed. Then, we talked for a while, and she turned over and went to sleep."

"Are you serious? I'm supposed to be getting calls saying that someone is banging against the wall by now." She laughed.

"Exactly! So, beautiful, what's your name?"

"My name is Punkin."

"Well, hey, Punkin. I'm Monta!"

Punkin looked surprised when I told her my name. "Wow, really? My friend was just talking about you the other day. She was saying that you had a daughter by her cousin."

"Oh, really? Well, I guess you know the tales then, huh?"

"Oh, do I... Man, if you only knew the things I've heard about you! Now, I guess it's my time to find out if it's true or not," Punkin said seductively.

"Maybe it is. Here take my number and call me sometimes. I mean like tomorrow if you're not too busy." I walked off, heading back up to the room.

Miya was sitting up in the bed when I returned. I removed my clothes and lay beside her with my eyes closed. She leaned over and kissed me. And that woke up the beast, so I kissed her back. Her lips sank into mine, and she fell into my arms as I undressed her with my eyes. I began kissing her softly, sucking on her neck, and making her body go crazy as I undressed her and dove right in.

My tongue explored her pussy lips, sucking on her clit, driving her crazy as I picked her up off the bed. Her pussy was still in my mouth as her body went limp, and her legs started shaking. I laid her down on the bed, still sucking on her clit. She came, gripping my head, body shivering, and shaking as she lost her mind to the best head ever. She couldn't take it anymore, so she ran right off the bed onto the floor with her legs still weak.

I picked her up and put her back in bed with my dick hard as ever. I put the head in just to see if it was okay or if it was too tight. As I stroked, she squeezed me tightly, and her eyes rolled to the back of her head. As she bit her lip, I could see the pain in her face. My strokes were slow and gentle. As I kissed her neck. I could tell that she never had anyone to pay attention to her body the way that I did. She came to the motion of some real lovemaking, and the scene would forever play in her head. When we reached an ending point, I wanted to leave something for her mind to wonder about. The music we made was awesome.

She got up and cleaned herself, and I followed. We laid in bed until our eyes closed. The next morning, we got up, put our clothes on, and checked out. We stopped and got some breakfast. Although it was sad to say it, it was time to split ways.

She looked me in the eyes and asked, "Where do we go from here?"

"Wherever here take us, beautiful. So, what? You want to be my lady?" I asked her.

"Only if you want to be my man, Monta."

"I would love to be your man, sweetheart."

We said farewell and went our separate ways. I was thinking that maybe she could take the place in my heart that Precious held for so long. I hung out every weekend with Miya and talked to her all day, every day. Months passed, and our feelings grew. We started spending more and more time together.

On October 28th, we were on the phone talking, and she got the feeling that she needed to feel what love was all about. We made plans to meet up when she got off work. As our workday came to an end, she called me and said she had to go home and change and that she had a surprise for me. I showered, got dressed, and headed over to my sister's house where my brother and a few guys were hanging out. Miya called and said she was on her way. I told her where I was and waited for her to show up.

The guys and I talked about a race and the rematch that we were going to set up. I could see Miya bending the corner, so I told the guys I would see them later, and me and Miya went to our destination. As we walked through the door, she went into the bathroom. Five minutes later, the door swung open, and standing in the doorway was a beautiful four foot eleven, sexy angel in a red lace lingerie with some gold heels that made my night lights come on.

The mood was on go, and everything was nice and slow. The scene was so hot that the walls were sweating. Her body was in a place she never thought could be possible as she trembled. I could feel her soul float up and through the room from the soft touch of my hands. My lips to her naked skin caused her to make a love face, and as she released her emotions, her eyes rolled to the back of her head. Biting her lips, she seemed to find herself.

When our session ended, we lie there, talking a while before we headed out. She had work in the a.m., and so did I. We went back to my truck, and I kissed her goodnight and watched her drive away. A few weeks went by. We'd talked off and on and hung out most weekends, but one night in November, she called and said we should see other people. I said okay and left it at that. The following week, I got a phone call from Miya saying that we had to talk.

"What is it that we have to talk about? You said what you had to say, so let's leave it at that," I told her in a dry tone. I didn't really see the point in having another conversation with her if she wanted to see other people.

"Monta, I'm pregnant," she said the words that made my mouth drop and my heart skip a beat.

Just last week, she said we should see other people, and I was trying to get to know someone else that I'd met. But now, after everything that had been said and done, Miya was pregnant. I wondered if I should see where this was going or just do as she requested and move on to someone else.

"So, Miya, when did you find this out?" I asked.

"Well, I took four tests. All four of the tests were positive."

"And you sure it's mine?"

"Monta, who the hell else would it be? I've been with no one but you!"

"So what do you want to do? I mean, you did say we should see other people, and I have met someone. But if you're pregnant, we have to handle this situation."

"Yeah, I know, but I don't know how to tell my parents," she said, sounding very familiar.

I was thinking, *Oh shit. Here we go with this again. Another grown-ass woman that has to have permission from her parents to have a child.* I tried not to let those thoughts come out in my tone when I asked, "So, Miya, why are you afraid to tell your parents that you're pregnant?"

"Monta, you don't know my parents like I do."

"What are you saying, Miya?"

"When they find out that I'm pregnant, they are going to put me out," she said.

"Well, you can just come stay with me. Hell, that's not a problem. That's if you want to. Just let me know what you want to do, Miya, okay?"

"I will, but right now, I'm just scared. That's all."

"I understand, sweetheart, but you don't have to be scared. I'm right here with you. Do you want me to tell them that you are pregnant?"

"No! I will do it. I just need a little time. That's all."

"Well, if you need me to help you or be there, I'm on it, sweetheart. I will call you tomorrow."

***

Weeks passed, and she still hadn't told her parents. One cold day in December, she called me crying her eyes out. "What's wrong, Miya?" I asked.

"They want me to have an abortion," she said as she cried.

"And what did you tell them?"

"I told them I didn't want to have one, and they said if I didn't have it that I would have to get out."

"Wow, really? Well, pack up your things and come on with me then."

"But they are not going to let me take my car."

"Are these motherfuckers slow or something? I mean, do they not know that you are a grown-ass woman? Well, get your stuff together. I will come and pick you up!" I said, not believing that her parents would take away her transportation, knowing that she was pregnant.

"No, Monta, I will just come tomorrow. It's late, and I don't feel good," she said softly.

The next day, Miya moved in. Things were going well until one night when she left her phone on the couch, and it rang. She told me to bring it to her, but by the time I got to the phone, it stopped ringing. A text came through, and it flashed up on the screen: *My dick missed you too!*

So, I opened the text she sent him, and it read: *I miss your dick.*

I closed out of the text, handed her phone to her, and went back into the living room and watched TV until my eyes got too heavy to stay open. I went to bed but stayed on my side and to myself. She turned over and wanted to have a conversation, but I didn't feel like talking, not to her anyway. I was thinking to myself that she must not know who I am. Well, it was game on since she was missing dicks and shit. It was time for me to put my other legs on and show her how a player works.

Days went by, and I still hadn't said a word. I went out one day and met a young lady by the name of Tish. We talked off and on, and one day, she called me and asked me what I was doing.

I told her, "Nothing. Just sitting at home watching TV. What you got going on?"

"Nothing. Just sitting here sick and out of work today," she said.

"So, you must be trying to trick me to Columbus to see you or something?" I asked.

"That would be nice, Monta. If you don't mind."

"Well, send me your address, and I will be there shortly."

Tish texted me her address, and I headed down the road to Columbus. As I was driving, my phone rang, and it was Crystal.

"Good morning, handsome. How are you?" she asked, sounding upbeat.

"I'm fine, sweetheart, and yourself?"

"I'm great. Just missing you."

"I miss you, too, beautiful. What's my son doing?"

Crystal said, "Growing and looking more like you every day. Monta, I'm ready to come home. I can't take this anymore. Does the offer still stand?"

"Well, baby, I have someone, and she's pregnant."

"Really, Monta! Why? Please tell me why you do me like that?"

"Look, baby, you allowed your parents to run your life. They sent you away because you were pregnant. What was I supposed to do, Crystal?"

"I guess nothing, Monta. You are every breath I breathe. Now you are telling me you have someone else, and she is pregnant. How do you think that makes me feel? I gave you everything that I had to call my own, and now you don't want it."

"Baby, I didn't say that. You know I wanted you, but I couldn't have you because you allowed your parents to control you. When I asked you to stay, you wouldn't. When you had our son, I tried to come and get you, and you didn't want me to do that either. What was I supposed to do? I couldn't keep waiting, wondering, and hoping for a long-time miracle. I love you, Crystal, I do. I wish you could have been here with me, but I guess things weren't meant to be, sweetheart."

"Monta, I don't want anyone else! You are the one who made my heart smile, and you're the father of my child. And now you are telling me that you don't want me anymore. You know what? You are no different! You're just like my parents.

Oh, and don't worry. Me and Delmonta will be just fine. I love you and always will, but this is goodbye!"

"But, Crystal!"

She hung up, so I decided to give her a little time. I pulled up to Tish's house and knocked on her door, which was three minutes away from where Whitney used to live. Out stepped a lovely, young lady with a beautiful smile and sexy everything else. I stepped inside, and Tish gave me a hug. We sat around and talked for a few hours until it was time for me to go. We said our goodbyes, and she gave me another hug.

On my way home, I got a call from a number I didn't recognize. The voice on the other end was shocking. It was someone I would have never expected to get a call from— Nora's daughter.

"Hey, Monta. How are you?" she asked.

"I'm fine, Mara, and yourself?"

"Well, I'm great, just a bit tired."

"What's wrong, sweetheart? Why are you tired?"

"I just had a long day. That's all. And I can't stop thinking about you."

"But why? It's been a few years now, so what is it to think about?"

"Monta, the way you took care of my mind and body was amazing to me. To this day, I can't keep a man because he can't do me the way you did me, and you weren't even my man! You were my moms, and we are still not speaking today. I don't go to family functions. She can't stand looking at me, and I don't give a damn. You should have been with me in the first place. Hell, we are the ones that are close in age, not you guys."

"Well, Mara. I hear what you are saying, but I think that was a mistake, and it was wrong on both our ends."

"I know, but I want you, Monta! I will come to you if I have to, but I have to see you."

"That will be impossible. I have a lady, sweetheart, and she is pregnant. I'm not trying to cause any more problems between you and your mom."

"I understand, but can I at least still talk to you sometimes?"

"That's fine. Well, I'm home, so I guess I will talk to you later."

"Goodnight, Monta. I pray that you have a change of heart."

"Maybe, I will. You never know, sweetheart. Goodnight, beautiful."

I went into the house, and just looking at Miya made me sick to my stomach, but I tried to push through it. I fixed something to eat and showered before bed. Our night was silent besides the TV being on.

Weeks passed, and me and Tish saw more and more of each other. I was at work one day when Tish called and asked if I would like to go to Wild Adventures that weekend with her and the kids.

"Sure, I would love to," I told her.

"We are leaving early Saturday morning, so you would have to come stay the night."

"Baby, that would be fine with me. You know I love to hold you at night," I said, and we talked a little while before I got back to work. The day went by smooth and fast. I got off work, went home, packed me a bag, and was out the door without even saying goodbye to Miya.

As I rode to Columbus, the radio in my Cutlass sounded off, bumping Eight Ball & MJG's "Comin' Out Hard" as I pulled up to Tish's house. We arrived at the same time, and she stepped out the truck looking all sexy with her short skirt and high heels. I put my bags upstairs, and my lips touched hers. It was like fireworks going off until the girls walked into the house.

We all went out to eat and watched a movie then headed to the house. We showered and got ready for bed. Tish put on a sexy black nightgown, and her curves made it fit so perfectly as the top sat beautifully on her breasts. I stared at the mountains of love before I dove into action and kissed her neck and then her lips. Then, I slowly found my way to her breasts that stood there so perfect and lovely. My lips tenderly caressed her nipples as she moaned and shivered. I knew my touch was everything she needed as I eased on down through the path of her curves.

As I reached her valley, I made her spring flow. Her moans got louder and louder, so I put the pillow over her face. As she reached her point of explosion, I slid my dick in her guts, and the music began. Every stroke was slow and deep. The passion and intensity filled the room. Sweat ran all over our bodies as I stroked her pussy while sucking her nipple. She came over and over again, scratching my back and biting her lips. The scene was so right I didn't even know I was cumming.

As we ended the session, we cleaned up and talked about the fun we were going to have at the park the next day. Before

I could kiss her goodnight, she was fast asleep. We were up early and getting dressed the next morning for the three-hour drive we had ahead of us. We loaded the truck and left for the park, stopping to get breakfast on the way. The ride was fun and smooth. We laughed and cut up the whole ride.

As we pulled into the park, Tish started feeling sick. I parked the car, and we sat there a while to see if she would feel any better. She didn't, so she told us to go ahead, and she would come later. Her kids and I went inside the park, and our time was awesome. They played and had fun on the rides. As we started to the animal park, Tish called me with some news that I was kind of thinking about myself. When she found us, she had a worried look on her face, so I asked her what was wrong. She said I will tell you when we get home, but first, we have to stop by Wal-Mart.

We continued through the park until everyone got tired. It was dark, and I was exhausted from the long day, so Tish drove home while me and the kids slept. She stopped by Walmart and grabbed a few things on the way home. As we reached the house, we all got out of the car and went up the stairs. We went into the bedroom, showered, and got ready for bed. She took a little longer than usual. After a while, I heard her cries and knew what it was.

She came out and said, "Go look," so I walked into the bathroom. She had taken both of the tests, and they both said she was pregnant. I was thinking to myself, *Man, if you don't cut your dick off and stop making these kids.*

We got closer as time passed until one day when Tish called Miya, and all hell broke loose. The crazy part was I was sitting right there when she called. I just didn't know who she was calling.

Miya left me after that confrontation. She had her friends come to help her move, and Tish held me hostage. When she finally let me leave, I went home to find that all my stuff and Miya's stuff was gone. I didn't care if she came back or not. I just wanted my things back. I was sitting in the house with no TV, just a remote and the TV stand.

I called Nora's daughter, Mara, and she invited me to her house, but I insisted we get a room. She got a room and gave me the address, and when I walked through those doors, it was a remake of the very first time. A beautiful Puerto Rican standing there wet from head to toe with a towel wrapped around her, starving for me.

"Monta, come get this pussy!" she said as if she had been craving this for a long time.

I picked her up, sat her on the sink, slid my rubber on, and we twelve played it for about three hours. From the sink to the floor, she came in every part of the room. Her pussy was still tight, juicy, and swollen from the strokes she begged so hard for. After a brief intermission, she climbed on top of me and rode the wheels off my ass.

With every motion, she squirted, and with every roll, she came. The climaxing took all of her energy. But I wasn't finished just yet, so I laid her on the bed and gave her the greatest sex she ever had, deep-stroking her pussy until I put her all in her feelings. Tears fell from her eyes as she begged me to stay with her forever. I went deeper and deeper, and she held me tighter while screaming my name.

"DAMN, MONTA! This dick is so fucking good and big, but don't stop baby. I need you inside me! Please get me pregnant!"

And that's when I changed modes and beat it down. I didn't need another baby. She wanted me to stay and hold her after we finished up, but I wasn't there for that. I went into the bathroom, washed up, and headed back to West Point.

As I traveled down 85, all I could think about was Precious and the fun we had during our time together. I never knew when thoughts of her would take over my mind and bring me back to her. To have a woman like that and allow her to slip through your fingers is a sin to your heart and soul. She was all any man could ask for, and I had her in my grip. The feeling I had was of a free bird. My wings could spread as wide as they needed to, and she would hold on for the ride. But that was over now. All I could do was wish and wonder.

When I was getting off the exit, I called Tish to see how she was feeling, and all I could hear was hurt and pain in her voice. I made it to the house and walked into a quiet, lonely house with no TV and no happiness.

The next day, Miya came back with my stuff, and to see the hurt in her face broke my heart. I don't know what kind of man she was used to, but I'm from across 85. I was trained as a cub that if a person treats me with respect and loves me right, then they wouldn't have a problem. If they hurt me once, then they better leave because I will grow ten legs. I took mine to a new level. A new meaning of being a dog and still loving you passionately at the same time.

"Hey, beautiful. How are you?" I asked Miya.

"I'm not good at all, Monta! I just came to bring your things back."

"Oh, okay. I will just get them and let you be on your way."

"Monta, why did you do that to me?"

"You did it to yourself. I saw that text where you and ole boy were going back and forth! You told him that you missed his dick, and he said you can get it whenever you wanted to."

"I was just making conversation. That's all."

"Making conversation isn't telling a man that you miss his dick, but it's cool. You can keep missing it because on this end I'm great!"

"Monta, I'm not thinking about that man. But why were you down that woman's house?"

"I was just trying to make conversation like you were."

"But she said that she was pregnant, so what's up with that?"

"Well, that's the conversation we were making."

"I'm having your baby. I need you to be here with us, not everywhere else. Just promise me that you won't see her again," Miya pressed the issue.

"That I can't do because there is a child involved in this situation," I said.

Knowing I was the only one Miya had at the moment, I had to take her under my wing. As bad as I wanted to leave her, being a man, I just couldn't see myself doing it.

As time went on, Miya got bigger, and so did Tish. Me and Miya got closer, and things were going okay, although our daughter was growing so fast that Miya barely could walk. Everywhere we went, I felt like I had a penguin with me. She was almost due, Shevonne just had our daughter in September, and Tish was due in December.

The summer came, and Miya had just moved back to Columbus. We were still moving along just fine, even though I hadn't forgotten about what happened between us. I was doing me, though, so when a beautiful Queen came along, I approached her and said, "Hey, beautiful, how are you?"

"I'm fine, and yourself?" she asked with a big smile, so I knew I had her.

"I'm great, sweetheart, but I would be a lot better with you on my arm."

"So you say!"

"And why shouldn't I say it? I say exactly what I mean, and I mean to get you."

"Oh, really? And how are you going to do that sir when you don't even know my name?"

"Yes, I do."

"What is it then, smart guy?"

"Mrs. Griggs."

"Real cute, but you have jokes!" she said.

"So, what is your name, or do I have to keep calling you Mrs. Griggs?"

"My name is Tina."

"Well, hello, Tina. I'm Monta, and I would love to get to know you better if that's not a problem with you."

"No, it's not a problem, funny guy. Besides, I love your sense of humor."

I laughed and told her, "But I promise I will get you to love more."

"And you have confidence, and by the way, I live in Texas so we won't see each other that much," she said.

"I will just have to make you fall in love with me and my conversation then," I replied, smiling.

"I hear you, Mister. Do you know I'm probably old enough to be your mother?" she asked.

"But the good news is you're not. I'm twenty-nine. If you don't mind me asking, how old are you?"

"I'm twelve years your senior," she said proudly.

"But you don't look a day over twenty, beautiful."

"Thanks, handsome."

I handed her my number I scribbled on a piece of paper. "Look, here is my number. Call me sometimes or maybe all the time."

She took the paper and put it in her purse. "I will do that, sexy!"

"Hey, you take care of that beautiful figure now."

"I will," she said and walked away with a sexy walk that could stop traffic.

That day, me and Miya talked off and on. She told me she had been in pain all day. In the back of my mind, I kind of figured she would be going into labor later that night or in the morning. After work, I went home, showered, and went to Columbus to check on her. I stayed awhile, caring for her, and then I headed back home.

As soon as my head hit the pillow, I was out cold. I was sleeping so hard that I didn't hear my phone ring. I finally heard a faint ring and noticed it was Miya calling to let me know she was on her way to the hospital. Her water broke, and I didn't know how much time I had before the baby would arrive. I pushed my foot through the floorboard, and that Cutlass floated all the way to Columbus.

I walked into her room, and the relief on her face was priceless. Even though we had problems, I just couldn't leave her alone and hopeless. I was the reason she was in the situation she was in with no one to turn to but me. When your parents turn their backs on you because you won't kill a child that you want, it is a hard and sad situation. My upbringing was pure, and love was endless, so I had to show her the same love I was taught to share by the greatest people I've ever known.

As the night went on, her pain grew, but no baby. The sun came up, and her doctor came in and gave her some hurry up and get your ass out here meds. The pains came on quicker, and my hand felt the pain of every contraction. As the pain got worse, it was time to push.

After five mins of pushing, my baby girl entered the world. The joy she brought into the room was unbelievable. Everything I had been praying for since August 31, 2007 had come to me in the form of a baby. To hold her and look into her eyes, I just knew my prayers were answered. She was Emma Brooks all over again.

As the doctor cleaned her up and took her away, I looked at Miya and said, "Thank you for giving me this blessing!"

"You mean *our* blessing," she corrected me.

"Yeah, that too."

They rolled Miya out of the delivery room and into her room, and I could hear my mom's voice saying, "I told you I would never leave you."

Chapter Thirteen

Miya slept as I played with our daughter until it was time for me to leave. I kissed my ladies and said goodnight. My smile had a new shape and brightness as I drove home, thinking deeply. My phone buzzed with a call from Tina that pulled me out of those thoughts.

"Hey, Monta, how are you?"

"I'm great, beautiful, and yourself?"

"I'm doing well, but I would be doing a lot better if I was in your arms right now!" Tina said.

"Oh, really?"

"Yes, I would, so can we make that happen?" she asked.

"When are you trying to get to me?"

"As soon as I can."

"So what you been doing all day, young lady?"

"Nothing much, just sitting around the house. I cooked dinner, and when I finished, I sat my ass on this couch and turned this TV on and been stuck ever since."

"Oh, so you're being lazy today, huh?" I asked.

"Well, not so much as being lazy. I'm just tired," she replied.

"I can understand that."

"So, what has your day been like, handsome?"

I told her, "Well, my baby was born this morning. Other than that, I haven't been doing anything."

"What did she have again?" Tina asked.

"She had a little girl, and she looks just like my mom. I mean just like her. I just hope she doesn't have that attitude like she had because that was a piece of work, baby."

"I bet she was. To deal with your bad ass, she had to be something."

"Really, Tina? So I'm bad now?"

"I hope so because you have to be to deal with me. I can be two handfuls!"

"I have some big ass hands, so I don't think you're ready for me." I tried to warn her.

"I hear you talking. I just hope you can back it up," she said, not knowing what she was in for.

"Oh, you will see pretty soon!" I told her.

"Monta, sing for me, please?"

"What do you want me to sing, sweetheart?"

"You can sing whatever comes to mind. I just love hearing your voice."

"So you like hearing my voice, huh?"

"Yes, I do."

"Well, maybe one day soon I can sing that song in your ear while painting on your canvas."

"My canvas? What do you mean by that?" she asked.

"Your body. See, a real man don't fuck nor does he have sex. A real man is an artist. He takes a woman and gently paints from her head to her valley below. Making her body feel the pleasure of his brush until he's painted a beautiful portrait, and she releases all the leftover paint that has aroused from the pleasure that he has given her."

"Damn, Monta! You just made me cum, and you're not even here! Wow! If it's that good through the phone, I can't wait to feel you in person."

"I told you I'm not like any man you have ever known. I'm the baddest thing since shoestrings."

"Well, okay then, Mr. Shoestring. I hear you. Now, I just want to feel you, so let's make sure that happens and real soon."

"I will talk to you later, beautiful." I hung up and made it to the house, showered, and got ready for bed.

Once in bed, my mind started to wander and think of what life would be like if I still had Precious with me. Would there have been anyone else carrying my kids? There were so many unanswered questions, so many different thoughts running through my head and heart at this moment.

The next morning, I woke up with a smile on my face, knowing my beautiful baby was coming home tomorrow. Joy flowed through my veins. Even though my heart was happy, my mind was still running with thoughts of what if...

I headed down the road to Miya's, and she called and asked my location. I told her, "I'm heading to you, baby."

"Well, can you stop and get me something to eat?"

"Yes, baby, I can do that. What do you want me to get for you, sweetheart?"

"Popeyes would do just fine and hurry up because I'm hungry."

"Look, just because you had my daughter doesn't mean you're the boss of me," I said.

"Monta, just hurry up and bring my food!"

"Yes, ma'am. I'm coming!"

I swung by Popeyes and picked up her food. I made it to the hospital, and my phone rang as I got on the elevator. The voice I heard on the other end was a voice I hadn't heard in a long time.

"Hey, Monta, how are you?" Whitney asked.

"Hey, Whitney. What are you doing? Have you talked to our baby?"

"Monta, she has grown so much, and she looks just like you. Well, to me, she does. Everybody else says she looks like me."

"I need to go see her and spend time with her and let her get to know her sisters and brothers," I said before adding, "Whitney, let me call you back."

"Okay, and you better call me back, too, Monta."

"I will, sweetheart," I said before I walked into the room where Miya and my daughter were lying in bed asleep. I woke Miya up and gave her the food she wanted.

"Thank you so much, Monta. I'm so damn hungry," Miya said.

"How has the baby been doing?" I asked, anxious to know more about my new baby girl.

"She's been shitting like crazy, and it stinks so bad," Miya complained.

I gave her a playfully stern look and said, "Don't be talking about my baby!"

"Well, it's true. She gets that mess from you."

"No, she didn't. I smell like strawberries!" I teased.

We talked and laughed for a while, and Miya slept off and on. Our day was so powerful; the energy was amazing. Her doctor came in, checked her and the baby, and let her know she could go home after he stopped by the next day.

"I'll go get her a car seat and see you in the morning."

"Okay. I love you, Monta."

"And I love you also, beautiful." I headed to West Point and went by Wal-Mart to grab a car seat. I made it to the house, showered, and got dressed for bed. I called Miya to check on her and the baby before I went to sleep.

"Hey, handsome, what you doing?" Miya asked.

"I just got in the bed and was thinking about you guys. What are you doing?"

"I'm watching the cooking channel."

"Oh, well, I love you, and I will be there in the morning," I told her.

"Monta, would you like to move to Columbus?"

"I don't know, baby. I mean, if you want me to, I will," I replied.

She said, "Well, when I get out tomorrow, we can go by and get an application."

"Okay, baby. We can do that. I love you, beautiful."

"I love you too, handsome. Goodnight."

I closed my eyes, and my thoughts went to work. Although my child was a joy to me, I couldn't stop thinking of Precious. My system wouldn't let her go for years. I tried to contact her but just couldn't reach her. No matter how hard I tried, I couldn't sleep. I would get a glass of water, drink it, and lay back down only to toss and turn until I finally fell asleep.

The next morning, I got dressed and headed to Columbus to the hospital. As I entered Miya's room, she was filling out paperwork, so I got the baby's stuff and took it down to the car. When I returned to the room, Miya's parents were there. Her father called me out in the hallway to talk, so we walked up the hall and stopped by the elevator.

"You know I don't like the fact that you got Miya pregnant. I don't think you're good enough for her. I don't like the fact that you have other kids either," her father said, and my mood changed up right then and there.

"Hold the fuck up! Now, I'm respectful because I was taught to be, but you don't know my kids or me, so you watch your damn mouth."

"I tell you what. Back in my day, I would have…"

"Back in your day? I'm still in mine, so we are going to leave this conversation alone. Because you're in the right place for me to fuck you up. I don't play about my kids, so this conversation is over," I said as he walked off.

There was an old couple at the nursery window looking at their grandbaby. The woman turned to me and said, "There you go, baby. You tell him because he doesn't have any business talking about your kids."

I headed back to the room, steaming about the way Miya's father tried to approach me. We got ready to leave, Miya asked what was said, so I talked to her about it.

"I know he didn't say that to you?" Miya asked in surprise. I assured her that her father had tried to play me in front of everyone in the hallway.

The nurse wheeled Miya out, and I went ahead to pull the car around. We put her and the baby in the car and headed to the house. We got the baby settled inside the house, and Miya reminded me about the application for the place she wanted to get. We talked for a while, and I headed back to West Point.

Eventually, I moved to Columbus in the new place with Miya. It was the first time I'd been out of West Point, and the feeling was great. As time passed, we were getting along well and enjoying our new space. We were having date nights and making family life really nice.

A couple months later, things were still going well until one morning around 3 a.m. when we heard a loud knocking sound back to back. Then, we heard someone running down the steps, and the door slammed. A few minutes later, there were flashing lights outside the window. I looked down and saw a deceased young man lying behind my car. My thoughts were that it was time to go. Two weeks earlier, a young lady was killed by her boyfriend on the right side of us, now this.

We moved across town, and things were going great. One night, Miya decided she wanted to go out with her friends. I was up cooking Sunday dinner after I got off work at 11 p.m., and as I was finishing dinner at 5:30 a.m., Miya walked in the house half-naked with a sweater on for a dress that looked like one of my tank tops. That's how short it was.

I asked her, "Why would you go out like that, and you are in a relationship? Don't you think that's kind of disrespectful? Just because your friends dress like they are single, you shouldn't out of respect for your man and yourself."

"Fuck you, Monta! Don't nobody have to have respect for your ass, and I'm grown!" Miya yelled.

"You're right. You're grown, and you're about to be single and grown."

We got into a scuffle, and things were said that shouldn't have been said. She decided that she wanted to go back to her folks. Later that morning, she was still upset, and the tension in the car was thick as we made it to church. As always, church was great. As the service went on, things got better, just a little. Afterward, we stopped by the store and headed back to the house.

Miya started packing her clothes with tears rolling down her face. I comforted her and wiped her tears as we made small conversation until her parents showed up to pick her up. As they walked out the door, I fixed a plate and had my dinner as planned. I didn't answer any of Miya's calls over the next few days. She came by to get more of her things, and we talked for a while. She couldn't stay long because her parents had her friend from across the street watching her to see what was going on as if she was a child.

I decided to move back to West Point, and on the day I started moving, Tish was having our son. I rushed over to the hospital and held her hands as she birthed my son. They had to take him early because of some complications. As they cut him out, I watched my son enter the world. He was so small, but my smile grew as they cleaned him up and took him away.

I stayed with Tish a while before I left the hospital and went back to the house. Miya called and asked what I was doing, and I told her I was headed to the house to finish packing.

"So you are leaving?" she asked.

I told her, "Yes, you ran back to your folks, and I only came here because you wanted me to."

"Can I come see you before you leave?"

"I guess you can if you want to. You know your friend is going to snitch on you," I said, but Miya wasn't worried about that.

I was upstairs packing when I heard her come in. Forgetting she still had her key, I grabbed my pistol, and then she bent the corner. She sat on the bed, and we talked while I packed. When I finished, she walked up to me and kissed me softly. I picked her up and laid her on the bed and sent my kisses deeper, passionately kissing her neck and making her eyes roll to the back of her head. She moaned, and I kissed on down and made her shiver. My tongue played a big part of our love scene. As I made love to her clit, her legs shook, and the force from her climax made her shiver more. Then, I slid my dick in so slow and gentle that the strokes were to die for. She moaned and screamed my name while we made music. The notes were at a perfect pitch, and the strokes were on key with slow passionate thrusts. She bit her lips with the sweetest love faces you would ever see.

As we got deeper into the scene, she whispered softly in my ear. "Damn, baby, your dick is good. I'm cumming, but please don't stop." I moved to the beat of her heart. Sweat dripped, and the room got hotter. We drifted off in space, making love like we never made before. I went deeper, and she screamed louder. "Yes, baby! Just like that."

I reached my peak, and she followed as we came together. We laid there talking, just enjoying each other after that great production. I had to get to West Point to get the truck to move my things, so we got cleaned up, and I walked her to the car and kissed her like I wouldn't see her again.

As I headed back to West Point, she called and said, "I hate that you are moving back, but I know you will always be here by my side."

"We all make mistakes, Miya. We just have to learn how to get up from them on our own. You have a family now, and your parents are not part of it. The sooner you learn that, the better your situations will be. I love you, and I will talk to you later, sweetheart."

I stopped by my sister, Lisa's, house and got Sam to help me. We picked up the truck and headed back down the road. We loaded the truck and trailer and went back to West Point. When we got to West Point, we stopped and unloaded the truck and trailer.

A few weeks went by. I got another place, and everything was going great. Miya came by. We went up to my dad's and hung out awhile. Then, she called me to the side and said she hadn't had her period yet, so we went to Wal-Mart and got a test. She went to the bathroom and took it. When she came out, she had tears in her eyes, so I already knew what the results were.

We went back to my dad's and sat in the car for a few minutes talking. She asked me not to tell anyone because she didn't know if she was going to keep it or not. The frustration on my face answered her without me opening my mouth. As we had a heated conversation about the situation, she broke down saying, "I don't want to disappoint my parents again."

"Fuck your parents! Are you their puppet or something?"

"No, I just don't want to upset them. They didn't want me to have Juicy. You know they are not going to let me have this one."

"What the hell you mean? They won't *let* you have anything. You're grown as hell. Y'all are some sick ass motherfuckers. Let me find out you aborted my baby, and y'all will have bigger problems!"

She got even more upset, and we left. I drove back to my place, got out of the car without a word, and went into the house. She called, and I didn't answer, so she left.

The next day, she called me, asking, "What are we going to do?"

"What you mean what we going to do?" I asked her with the same fire in my tone as I had the day before.

"I told you I'm not having this baby!" she said sternly.

I replied, "Man, get the fuck off my phone with that bullshit."

Apparently, she talked to her parents, and they told her to tell me that she took a test, and it was negative. So, one day, Miya came to the house with two tests, and we sat down and talked. She was trying to sell me that lie, but I had been in the streets too long for that dumb shit to get over on me. She had a bottle of water in her hand, so I figured she took a sip of water and went to the bathroom and spat on the test. Being me, I picked the test up, looked at it, and knew exactly what went down in the bathroom. I got the other test and said, "Now, let's go take this one together."

She broke down in tears. Right then, I knew it was all a game she and her parents were trying to play on someone that they thought was a dummy. She left, and I just sat there thinking about what the hell I had gotten myself into messing with this woman. Even as days and weeks went by, they were still trying to get her to abort the baby, but my muscle was bigger than they would have thought.

They kicked her out again, and she came to live with me. Our relationship was on the rocks, and I didn't really want her there. She didn't want to be there, but we had a situation at hand, so things had to work out for a moment. Then, on July 19th, as we were lying in bed, she kept crying and saying that her stomach was hurting. I rubbed her stomach for a while until she said it was better. She cried all night, and that next morning, July 20th, our daughter's birthday, I took her to the hospital.

Days went by, and she still hadn't given birth to our son. Then, on July 27th, she gave birth to a healthy boy. I embraced him with nothing but love. Miya was discharged from the hospital, and a week went by with everything being okay. The next week, she up and left, leaving our son behind. I cared for him, and when I had to work, my thirteen-year-old daughter stayed at the house with him, or my sister, or my ex-wife Shevonne had him. I made sure he was surrounded by love and all the support he would ever need.

Chapter Fourteen

I met Keila at the mall, and we hung out a while, getting to know each other until the night she felt lonely and horny. She called me up, and I rushed over and picked her up to bring her back to the house. I put some smooth jams on, and we enjoyed each other's company, laughing and cutting up. I turned the lights down low to set the mood just right. Keith Sweat came on, singing "Right and a Wrong Way" as I pulled her up to slow dance to the jam. I kissed her neck as we grew closer and hotter from the grinding. We made our way to the bedroom, and I picked her up and laid her on the bed.

Our clothes came off so quick and smooth that we didn't even know we were in bed making music. My dick spread her lips to the max. She screamed out, "You're too big. Please go slow." But my strokes went hard and slow as we fucked up my sheets. She squirted and squirted as her legs shook. She bit down on her lips and tapped out. She couldn't take it anymore.

We cleaned up, and she didn't want to go home, so she stayed the night. We laid in bed talking about the possibility of us becoming one, but I wasn't feeling that at the moment.

Waking up to a bird outside of the window singing love songs, we got up and got dressed. I took her home and headed to LaGrange before work. Walking through the mall, I met this fine young lady that went by the name Britt. We sat down and talked for a while, then exchanged numbers and went our separate ways.

I picked up what I needed and headed back to get ready for work. I made it to the house, and Britt called asking when she could spend time with me so we could get to know each other better. I said this weekend would be fine if I could find a babysitter. We talked every day and night that week, learning more about each other.

In the process, I met this young lady at work that was feeling me. Her name was Chondra. Chondra was a sweet, young lady, and her style was different. She had her own swag.

Friday, Britt called and said she wanted to take me out, so I met her in Auburn, and we hung out, went to the movies, and out to eat, then back to her apartment.

"So, Monta, how did you like our date?" she asked.

"I never had a woman take control the way you did. I mean, it's a first time for everything I guess."

"What kind of music do you like? Wait, don't tell me. Let me surprise you!" she said and put on some Johnny Gill "Take Me I'm Yours."

My mind took control. She stepped in her room and came out with some laced panties and a bra that set the freak in me on fire. We went from the living room to the balcony with clothes peeling off and things breaking. She started out like a wild woman until she saw the magic I had. Then, the calm came before my storm. She was five foot three and weighed one hundred and fifteen pounds. Her curves were like a dangerous road, and she wore heels that stood about nine inches off the ground.

As we made a movie scene outside, the stars and moon dazzled in the sky from the show that was put on. I pulled her to me and put her on my shoulder. Moaning and scratching, she came and came, begging me to fuck her over the rails. I bent her over, put my rubber on, and slid my dick in slow and easy. The way her pussy screamed when I started stroking should've woke the neighbors on both sides of us. She begged for it harder. As I went deeper, she fell to the floor with her hands clutched to her stomach.

I picked her up, slid her back on my dick, and fucked her from the balcony to the bed. Squirting, she screamed, "Keep fucking me like that, daddy. Damn, this dick is big and great at the same time. Pull that rubber off and put that dick back in me." The strokes got so good that she wouldn't let me pull out. Her legs shook, and she kept asking, "What are you doing to me? Why won't my legs stop shaking?"

It was time to really fuck her head up, so I pulled it out slowly and went back even slower, sending her into space. Her eyes rolled to the back of her head, and tears leaked out of the corners as she closed them. She had reached her destination, so I kept my pace and made the strokes cater to her insides while I sucked on her beautiful nipples. As she came and got lost in the moment, tears fell, and her sheets got wetter. My dick went deeper, and she wrapped her arms around me.

At that point in the session, I had her right where I wanted her. This little mixed Puerto Rican/Asian princess had all of Monta in her, and she couldn't let go.

Checkmate.

Britt looked in my eyes and said, "Monta, I love you. Please, don't let me go! Monta, I'm about to cum."

That was my key to catch that moment with her. I went deep and strong, hitting that point of no return as we reached the peak of the night. Afterward, we just laid there with her crying as she snuggled up in my arms.

"I don't know what you did to me, but I can't get control of myself. That's the first time I've ever made love, and you did it like it was no tomorrow. You knew every spot to hit and how to grind at the moment that I needed it. It was like you knew my body better than I knew my own self."

"See, that's my job to master your body and collect your soul."

"I swear, Monta, that is what you did. I don't even feel like the same person anymore. The way your dick just took over my pussy was like damn man. That shit is so big. Can I get it in the morning? That is the best sex ever!"

"Yeah, it might be, but I don't have sex. I make music."

"You're right. We just made two albums then. I promise you."

We fell asleep with her in my arms. The next morning, I awoke to her hands pulling on my dick like it was a lawnmower cord.

"Let's get this thing started up, baby," she said.

Knowing that I had to go, we did a quick remix of last night, and she cooked me breakfast and fed me really well. I jumped in the shower, and she followed me to get round three. She bent over and got in a stance that I couldn't refuse, so I slid my dick in her doing long, slow strokes. In the middle of going deep, someone opened the bathroom door and in walked a beautiful, dark-skin goddess. My strokes didn't stop as she stood there watching. She dropped everything in her hands and slowly pulled her panties off while playing in her perfectly shaven pussy lips.

The dark-skinned goddess stepped in the shower, pulled my dick out of Britt, and licked and sucked on my dick like it was a hot summer day, and she had a bomb pop. In and out, stroking it and shoving it deep down her throat.

Britt got a rubber out of the drawer, slipped it on my dick, and shoved it into her roommate's tight pussy. She screamed and ran, but Britt pushed her back harder. As I went deeper and deeper, the goddess fell to the floor, so I flipped her on her back and stuck it back in. The fun began as I stroked her tight, wet pussy harder and harder. She begged and pleaded as she scratched my back as she came.

I was in the best place a man could ever dream of, destroying not one but two of the prettiest women you would ever see. As the scene started coming to an end, I stood up and let them enjoy the taste of my cum. They both washed me. Then, we got dressed and said our goodbyes.

As I got to the house, I got dressed for work, fixed my lunch, and went to work. The first smile I saw when I entered the building was Chondra's.

"Hey, Monta, how are you today?"

"I'm fine beautiful, and yourself?"

Me and Chondra had been talking for a while now, and things were going good, so I replied, "I'm better now that I've seen you."

"Monta, are you going to the pub tonight?"

"Yes, ma'am!"

"Well, I'm going too since you're going."

"So, you want to be with me tonight? Is that what you're saying?"

"Well, you can say that!"

"I will be there then."

"Just make sure you're not dancing with no other chick when I walk in."

"Sweetheart, I don't dance. I just sit back and watch."

"So you are looking for you a victim then, I see."

"Well, you will be my victim tonight," I said.

My shift came to an end, and we cleaned up and hit the clock. I hurried home to shower, check on my baby, and head to the pub. The scene was jumping. The crowd was lit, and the ladies were right. I found my crew, grabbed me a seat, ordered a cup of water, and enjoyed the show. I looked up and saw Chondra staring me down. She walked over, snatched me up, and took me to the dance floor. R Kelly's "Sex Weed" came on, and she put on a show. Seeing her at work, I didn't think her body could move like that, but I was wondering if she could move like that between the sheets.

As the night went on, we hung out, and she never left my side. The night came to an end, and we all went outside. She told her friend that she was going home with me, so she followed me to the house. From the front door to the bedroom, it went down. She climbed in bed, and I followed her. The kissing began, clothes flew off, and the valley was open, so I dove in. The motion she had was clearance that neither her head nor her body was ready for what I was about to do to her. My lips grabbed her clit, and my fingers found the entrance to her tight pussy as we wrote the script to the leading act. She moaned and moaned as she grabbed my head, pushing it back as she came.

"Damnit, Monta! That felt so good," she screamed as she pulled me up. "Put it in!" She was ready for the music to begin, so I slid the head in. She jumped from the width of his entering, and I pushed it on in. She stuck her fingers into my back, screaming, "It hurts."

Slowly, I stroked and stroked deep in her pussy as she lost control of herself with her legs shaking and pussy skeeting as I stroked strong and slow.

"Monta, I'm about to cum!" she yelled as she wet my sheets. Her pussy was wet and sloppy, so I stroked harder, picking up the pace and going deeper and deeper. Her scream rang through the house. "Monta, it hurts. Slow down!" she said with tears rolling down her face. So I dove deeper, reaching the peak of my nut and exploded.

We cleaned up and talked for a while before she left. As I walked her to her car, she turned around and gave me a kiss, saying, "I love you, and I want something serious with you, so please don't hurt me."

I opened her door and saw her off. I ran back upstairs and got me a shower and laid down. I was beginning to close my eyes when my phone rang. As I answered it, I heard the voice of an angel say, "Hey, Monta, what you doing?"

"Just got in bed. What are you doing up this late at night?"

"I was just thinking about you, wishing I could see you."

"Britt, it's late, and I have to get up early in the morning."

"I just want to lay in your arms, Monta. We don't have to do anything. I just like the way you make me feel secure, that's all."

"Well, come on, baby. You know I can't say no to you with your sexy ass."

Thirty minutes later, my doorbell rang, and I opened the door to Britt and her roommate. They walked in, looking like two movie stars. We went to the bedroom, and as she said, they both laid in my arms and went to sleep.

Around 6:00 a.m., I was awakened by warm lips wrapped around my little head and the feel of the back of Britt's roommate's throat. She put her finger up to hush me as she grabbed my dick and pulled, getting me out of bed as she stepped into the bathroom and stepped into the showers. She threw a leg on my shoulder and slid my dick in her perfect, wet lips. I went deep and could feel the warmth of her pussy as it creamed all over my dick. She bit her lips as I stroked slow and quietly. I only stroked harder and deeper when she begged for it. She moaned and bit down on her lips harder as she squirted and squirted. Her legs shook and got weak. She tried to hide her pain, so I turned her around and spread her cheeks and went in from the back. Her moans were louder in this position, and it wasn't long before the door swung open and in stepped a half asleep and very pissed off half Asian and half Puerto Rican.

Without a word, Britt pulled my dick out of her roommate and shoved it into her mouth, sucking and slurping.

"Round two, I guess, ladies?"

"Hell, no! This bitch is getting out and getting out now! Monta, how are you going to just wake up and give her the dick, and you are with me?"

"You better get your ass in this tub and hush before I send you both home."

"I don't want to do it in the shower. I want you to make love to me. Now, dry off and come on, and this bitch is going to watch."

I stepped out of the shower and into the bedroom. The way that room held my secrets was amazing. I know the neighbors could hear the sounds that were made from two blocks away. As I was buried deep in her pussy, I waved her roommate over and laid her under us. Out of one and into another, that day, I felt like a king all over again. I could tell these tales for years and years to come, and it would never get old.

Once we were all satisfied, they showered together as I cleaned my room and then saw them off. In the back of my head, thoughts of Precious would always linger, no matter how many women I slept with. I still couldn't find what we had together.

I showered, got my things together for work, and headed out to work where I ran into a beautiful, thick snow bunny. She smiled, and I knew I had her, so we talked and exchanged numbers then walked our separate ways. That was a good thing because Chondra was headed towards me, asking, "What are you doing talking to that bitch, Monta?"

"Man, hush. We was just speaking. Don't make me beat you and her."

"Okay, baby. I won't. Now, what you bring us to eat?"

"I brought you something to eat, alright. But I will order us something if you can get somebody to go get it for us."

I ended up sending someone to get our food, and we sat in the breakroom and ate together. As I looked up from my plate,

Tonya was staring at me with a smile. I received a text from her saying: *Can I come and lick the sauce off your fingers.*

We texted back and forth throughout the day, smiling as we passed each other. As the workday came to an end, I cleaned up and headed to the clock. I felt a tap on my shoulders, and it was Chondra.

"Hey, Monta, you want to come stay the night with me?"

"I would love to, sweetheart. Let me go home and get a shower and get some clothes."

"Okay. I will see you when you get there, baby."

I went home, showered, grabbed some clothes, and headed out the door. As soon as I hit the interstate, my phone rang. On the other end was a voice I hadn't heard in a while.

"Hey, Monta."

"Hello, Crystal. How are you and my son?"

"We are great. It's not like you care."

"Look, man, don't ever play me like that. You took my son away, and when I asked you to move with me, you put it on your parents, so miss me with that bullshit."

"Anyway, I was just missing you and wanted to hear your voice. That's all. You know I still love you, right?"

"Really? What is it that you love about me, Crystal?"

"Monta, you taught me a lot. You showed me how to be a woman and gave me the most precious gift ever, our son. He is you all over again, Monta. He looks and acts just like you. Del is bad as hell. Do you hear me, but he really listens and understands what an ass whipping is."

"So, you be whipping my baby?"

"Hell, yeah, I do. This boy is so destructive and strong!"

"So, when am I going to see you guys?"

"We will be home in two more weeks. I will make sure you see us, okay, baby?"

"I hear you. Look, I will call you later, beautiful. I love you."

I got out of the truck and went into the house. Chondra had me a plate on the table and my favorite drink waiting on me.

"I've been waiting for you, handsome, so we could eat and go to bed."

"After I eat this, I can't do nothing but go to bed."

We laughed, ate, and watched TV a while before we headed to bed. She jumped in the shower and came to bed, smelling like a fresh bucket of "hello" and "get over here." I went in, kissing her all over as she pulled me close. I slid my dick inside of her and went to work, trying not to be loud.

She cried out, "Monta, don't get me pregnant!"

"I won't. I promise you."

As the session came to an end, we got cleaned up and laid there talking for a while before she fell asleep. My phone rang, and it was Tonya.

"Hey, Monta, what you doing?"

"Nothing. Just laying here. What you doing?"

"I'm laying here horny and naked, and I would love some company. Well, actually, your company, so come and be that for me."

I jumped up, put my clothes on, and told Chondra I had something to do and that I would call her later. She walked me to the door and kissed me goodnight, and I headed over to Tonya's. I arrived at her house, and as soon as I walked in, closed the door, and locked it, she was standing there in her birthday suit. Every curve was in the right place. She grabbed my hand, led me to her room, and we climbed in bed. She pulled me close, kissing me all over my chest and neck. I sucked on her breasts as she lost control of herself.

In the back of my mind, something kept telling me don't do it, and when my conscious speaks, I listen. So we laid there, and she laid on my chest and fell asleep. I woke up around 5:30 that morning and headed home. On my way home, my heart cried, and my mind wandered, thinking about my lost time with Precious. No matter what went on or who I met, I couldn't stop thinking about her. Only a person that's in love would understand my thoughts and cries.

Eventually, Chondra moved on, and so did Tonya. We still spoke off and on, but that was all.

Chapter Fifteen

Weeks rolled by. One day I was standing at the rail and up walked a beautiful, chocolate goddess with a smile so bright and teeth white as snow.

"Hey, beautiful, how are you?"

"Hey, I'm fine, and yourself?"

"I'm great, just struck by the beauty you carrying. So are you taken?"

"No, I'm not. You must be trying to take me?"

"Maybe, if you're takable, 'cause I'm in the taking business."

"Well, here is my number. Call me sometimes, and we can work that out. By the way, I'm Key."

"Okay, Key. I'm Monta."

"It's nice to meet you, Monta."

"Likewise, beautiful!"

Key and I started talking and getting to know each other, and she had a friend who wasn't feeling that process. One night, Key came into work early and asked if she could get my parking spot. I went outside and moved my truck, so she could park. I sat in the car with her a while before we walked in the building. As we got ready to get out of the car, she leaned over and kissed me on the lips, not knowing my lips would hypnotize her. She fell deep into a trance as I licked her bottom lip and made her body shiver. I pulled away, and she pulled me back even closer. Knowing what would happen if we went any further, I pulled away and stepped out of the car. It took her a minute to get out because she lost her legs in that kiss. I helped her out the car, and we walked inside the building.

My shift was already over, so we said our goodbyes, and she walked on. Every evening that week, we had to repeat the first day. If Key worked over or not, she wanted a kiss. This night, she took off so she could go home with me. She followed me home, and I took a shower and fixed us dinner. We ate and watched TV, but as the night winded down, she got sleepy, and we headed to bed. She laid in my arms and kissed me on my jaw and then moved to my lips. As I kissed her back, I could feel the trembling in her body. The kisses got deeper, and she reached down and grabbed my dick. The reaction she had let me know she wasn't ready, so I didn't force her into doing anything. I just laid there and held her while she slept.

The next morning, I cooked her breakfast, then got ready for work and saw her out. I was walking her to her car when she looked at me and said, "I'm sorry about last night."

I replied, "It's okay. Anacondas run in the family."

We both smiled. I kissed her, and she drove off. So I went back upstairs, gathered my things for work, and headed out to work. I stopped at the store to grab some gum, and Miya called.

"Hey, Monta, how you doing?" Miya asked.

"I'm fine, and you?"

"I'm doing great. Just had you on my mind."

"Oh, okay, so what were your thoughts?" I asked.

"I'm about to move in my own place."

"That's great. I'm proud of you!"

"Thanks."

"So, you want me to move down there with you?" I asked.

"I don't know…"

"Well, I will call you later. I'm at work now, Miya."

"Okay. I love you, Monta."

"I love you also, Miya."

After I hung up, I thought about whether I should move back in with Miya. My heart was saying, "Don't do that, stupid. You just got out of that hole; don't climb back into it."

I ignored my heart and followed my mind. I moved back to Columbus with Miya. Things were going well until one day when she told me to go to West Point and hang out with my friends. I just looked at her as if I didn't know what was going on. I knew people in higher places and could get any information I wanted at any time.

My alter ego told me to go to the mall for a while and wait until she came back and then show them who the fuck you are. My higher conscious told me it wasn't worth it. So I let her know that I knew she was talking to someone else and that they had planned a day together, so I was to go to West Point for the night. The look she gave me was priceless. I should have kicked myself in the ass for moving back in with Miya, but it was time to turn the hoe in me back on.

A few days later, I meet a beautiful young lady at the mall by the name of Jennifer. We exchanged numbers and got to know each other. As time passed, the talks got deeper, and our conversations got more personal. One Friday, we made plans to get together, so I got off work and headed down Jennifer's house. As I pulled into the driveway, Miya called.

"Hey, where are you?"

"I'm still in West Point. What's up?"

"I just wanted to talk to you, that's all."

"Well, I will call you when I leave."

"Oh, okay. Well, I guess I will talk to you then."

I got out the car and rang the doorbell. Jennifer answered the door, wrapped her arms around my neck, and placed a wet kiss against my lips as she pulled me in the house.

"Wow! I like that introduction! Does everybody get that when they come over?"

"No, sir. You are the only man worthy of that. After hearing your voice for so long, I think it's time for me to give you what I have been telling you about."

"What, that little weak ass pussy you been bragging about? Look, let me tell you about us across 85 guys. We don't play, so speak wisely."

"I don't care where you from. I promise you can't handle me, young man."

I quickly shut her mouth as we started painting. Her body showed me every thought that went through her mind as she lost control of her legs and mind with fluids running out all over her sheets. I slid my dick in, and her pussy was full and took it all. She screamed and clawed my back with tears falling as she begged for mercy. The louder she screamed, the deeper I went, and the harder I stroked.

As the session came to an end, we were drenched with sweat and her juices. She couldn't move, so I got up and turned the shower on. I took a shower and got dressed. Her legs and body were still weak from that 85 beat down she said she could handle. Being the man I was, I sat on the bed and talked to her until it was time for me to head home.

"Hey, sweetheart. I'm about to head out. Are you going to walk me to the door?"

"Really, Monta? I can't even feel my legs, and you want me to get up?"

"Well, little girl, I guess I will lock your door then."

"I guess you will. Are you going to call me and let me know you made it home safely?"

"I can do that," I said and headed home.

As I pulled in the yard, my phone rang. It was Jennifer checking on me. "Baby, have you made it home yet?"

I smiled. "Yes, baby, I just pulled in the yard."

"Well, okay. Goodnight," she said.

I had to ask, "Have you made it to the shower yet?"

"Nope, not yet. I'm still laying in the same spot that I was in when you left."

"Poor baby. I bet you watch what you say to me from now on, won't you?"

"Boy, get off my damn phone!"

"Goodnight, Jennifer."

As time passed, me and Jennifer got closer. One day I was at work, and she called me with some sobering news. "I'm pregnant, Monta."

"How, baby? I wore a jimmy hat, and it was super tight."

"Look, crazy-ass boy, this is not a time to be silly."

"I'm sorry, baby. Are you okay?"

"Yes, I'm fine, but all my kids are grown, and now I'm starting back over again!"

"Well, you will have me with you this time," I said to console her.

Later that day, I was making my rounds, and this young lady was walking to the time clock with her man. He was talking to her like shit, so I motioned for her to come to talk to me. She came over, and I asked her, "So, why are you allowing that lame-ass dude to talk to you like that?"

"I just don't have time to argue tonight, that's all."

"Let me wipe all those problems away for you, sweetheart."

"And how are you going to do that?"

"Just let me show you."

"I will be in early tomorrow, and we can talk then," she said.

My shift ended, and I headed to Columbus. As I was driving, my phone rang. It was Tina. "Hey, Monta, what you doing?"

"I'm just getting off and headed to the house. And what are you doing, sexy lady?"

"I was just laying here thinking about you."

"Oh, yeah? So, what were you thinking?"

"I'm ready to see you, so you can sing in my ear like you promised."

"Believe me, baby, I got you covered. You feel me?"

"Not yet, but I'm ready to with your little young sexy ass. I was telling my friend that I found me a young man the other day. And she was saying you just want to mess that baby head up. And I was like this one is different. I think he has that old school granddaddy pimp in him."

"Baby, you crazy. You better not be trying to give me the damn worms either because I promise you I will fish with them motherfuckers."

"Boy, you crazy, but I like it, and I like you."

"Well, let me call you back, sweetheart. I'm about to go in the house."

Once inside, I showered and fixed me a plate. Then, I watched TV until I got sleepy. I woke up the next day around 11 a.m., got ready for work, and headed to West Point. I made it to work and walked in with my cousin, Arthur, talking about last night.

"Monta, you got her, cuz. She wants you. You pulled his ticket in his face, and that shit turned her on. You're going to make Chondra and Tonya whip your ass and that girl on third shift."

"Who Key, cuz? She can't do anything. Her friend got her tied down. She can't even look this way anymore." I started my workday as I changed my battery on my tugger. I saw Tip working, so I pulled over there and spoke. "Hey, beautiful. How are you?"

"Hey, handsome. I'm good. What you doing over here?" Tip asked.

"I saw your sexy ass over here, so you know I had to come talk to you."

"Oh, I told your daddy that I was going to take all of your money like I do everybody else in here," she said.

"Baby, trust me, I'm not these dudes. I will have you eating out of my hands, I promise you!"

"Boy, I will put this on you and have your whole life messed up. I'll have Danny and Tia trying to fight me," she said, talking about my father and sister.

"Okay. I hear you. Just watch me work," I said to her. "So, what's your name?"

"My name is Tip. What's yours?"

"Well, it's good to meet you, Tip. I'm Monta, the man who will change your mind on the whole player role."

"Damn, boy, you smooth. I might not need to fuck with you."

"I'm trying to tell you. I come with a warning sticker like that song say, play at your own risk! So that's what I'm talking about," I said, warning Tip.

"I'm about to go talk to your daddy about you. I don't know about this," she said.

From that conversation, me and Tip started going out and talking more. One night, we were sitting in my truck outside her house talking, and the conversation got deeper than she expected. She got in her feelings, and tears started to roll down her face as she held my hands and expressed how she felt.

"Monta, I have never met anyone like you. You took your time and got to know who I was and didn't try to get in my pants just because I have a big ass. Do you know how much that means to a woman... well, to me? And you actually sit and have a nice and interesting conversation that doesn't have anything to do with sex. Monta, I'm falling in love with you, and I can't control it! Boy what are you doing to me?"

"I'm doing what I told you I would do, and that's be real with you. I told you that I was something that you wasn't ready to get to know just yet. See, when I get your attention, that's what I do, get your attention from the inside out. The best way to win a woman's heart is from the inside, not from the outside. Sex is easy to do, but it takes a real man to master making love. That's by making her soul love you first and then her heart. When you first touch her, that mind and body belong to you and only you."

"Wow! I'm ready to see how that feels. The way you make it sound, I know it has to be awesome." She leaned over and kissed my lips, and I kissed her back, giving her body chills that I could see rising on her skin.

We got out of the truck and went into the house. I put on my playlist and laid her down, kissing her softly, but this kiss wasn't like all the other kisses. This was a special kiss. A kiss that had feelings and passion that my heart could feel. I slowly moved down her body, reaching her breasts, and the attention I gave them was incredible. I took my time with the swirl of my tongue, gently sucking from one side to the other.

As she bit down on her lip, I moved on down further, giving every inch of her body my undivided attention until I reached her unique pussy lips. I placed my tongue on her clit and casually massaged it while sucking gently. She arched her back, moaning as she scratched mine. I grabbed her legs and pulled her closer as she came.

My tongue drew a perfect portrait. She grabbed my head to push it away, but I wasn't done with the artwork. There was something about this canvas that had me in my feelings, and I just couldn't figure it out. I was almost done. I just had to touch it up a little more before the music began. So, I flicked my tongue to make her pussy wetter before I slid my dick in. I eased forward, smacked her pussy with the tip of my dick, and gently slid in.

The tightness of her lips was like fire from a blazing flame, but the way they embraced it was amazing. As my strokes began, Tank slowly leaked out the speakers of my phone, and we got lost in the scenery.

I could hear her voice softly saying, "Monta, what you doing to me? Why does this feel so good? I love the way you are loving on me. Please don't stop, Monta. I'm cumming!"

I went deeper and could feel every pulse her body made. I moved to the beat, and with every insertion, my dick fell in love. The strokes got stronger, and we reached our peaks at the same time as we exploded together. We just laid there, and our minds went to places we never knew existed as we talked about our night. She laughed as I joked about her facial expressions. As time crept upon us, I had to get down the road so I could get ready for work the next day. She walked me to the door and hugged me like it was our last time together. I kissed her goodnight and headed home.

Miya was sitting on the couch, so I sat down beside her. She looked at me and said, "Monta, my period hasn't come on."

"Go take a test," I said because I knew she had a few kits in the bathroom. She proceeded to take the test, and I waited patiently. A few minutes later, I heard her cries, and I already had my answer.

Weeks later, Tip and I were still going strong, and things with Miya were the same. One Saturday evening, I got a call from Miya saying she had a pain in her side and stomach that wouldn't go away. We went to the emergency room, where they checked her out and told her she had a miscarriage.

The next day, I stopped at the Circle K to get gas, and as I stepped out the truck, a beautiful young lady pulled up at the pump beside me. She got out of her car and walked into the store to pay for her gas. Her movements and beauty froze me where I stood. As she walked back out, my eyes followed her from the store to the pump. I rushed over and grabbed the gas nozzle, and began to pump her gas. Forgetting that I was heading to work, we held a conversation and exchanged numbers. I opened her door, let her step in her car, and kissed her hand. Her cheeks turned red as she smiled and drove away.

I pumped my gas and headed to work. Five minutes into my drive, my phone rang, and it was her. "Hey, you know, out of all that talking, we didn't really introduce ourselves, so hello. My name is Shay," she said.

"Hello, Shay. I'm Monta. It was nice to meet you."

"And it was nice to meet you also, Monta. So where you from?"

"I'm from West Point."

"Oh, okay. Well, I'm from Florida, but I've been in Columbus for five years. I have a house down here and one in Alpharetta."

"That's great, so the magic question is, are you single?" I asked.

"Well, I gave you my number, didn't I," she snapped.

"Yes, ma'am, you did."

"So, are you single, mister?"

"Well, I'm not going to lie. I'm not single."

"You are too much of a gentleman to pass up, and you're sexy as hell."

"I'll call you later, Shay. I just made it to work."

"Okay, make sure you text or call me, Monta. I would love to know more about you."

"I will, beautiful. I promise." I got out of the truck and started walking to the building when I heard a voice calling out to me. I didn't see anyone, so I continued walking.

Later that night, when it was time for the next shift to come in, I was standing at the front with the guys when I felt a tap on my shoulder. I turned around and got an earful of Key screaming at me.

"Why you didn't come when I was calling you today?" she yelled.

"Because I didn't see who was calling me, and I was running late, so I didn't have time to stop."

"You've been acting funny since you fucking Tip, I see!"

"It's not that. Anyway, didn't your friend tell you to stop messing with me?"

"I'm grown, and don't nobody tell me what to do!"

"Well, why did you stop talking to me then?"

"Because I did!"

"Well, keep that trend going. Poof, be gone." I headed out the door, and my phone buzzed with a call from Shay.

"Hey, Monta. You off yet?"

"Yes, I just walked out the door."

"What are you about to do?"

"About to head that way. What's up?"

"I wanted to see you if that's okay with you. Can we make that happen?"

"I think we can work that out."

I headed down 103, listening to Jagged Edge. I was thinking about the mess I was getting myself into by playing with all these different hearts. My phone rang, and on the other end was a weak cry from Jennifer.

"What's wrong, sweetheart?"

"I just had a miscarriage, Monta. I've been in the hospital a week. I wanted to call you, but I just didn't want to bother you. I haven't talked to you in months, so I just left you alone."

"Why didn't you call me? I don't care what I had going on. I would have been there with you, Jennifer!"

"I didn't want no one but you, Monta, but I just couldn't bring myself to call you. My mom and kids asked me why I didn't call you, and every time they called your name, all I could do was cry."

"Baby, I'm sorry I wasn't there for you. Is it anything you need?"

"Yeah, I would like to have our son back!"

"So, it was a boy?"

"Yes, they showed him to me."

"Wow, and I wasn't there when you needed me most."

"Could you come to see me tomorrow, Monta?"

"Yes, I will. What room you in?"

"I'm in room 306 and bring me something to eat when you come, please. I'm tired of this nasty ass food they keep bringing me."

"I will call you when I get up in the morning and get ready to head your way. I love you, Jennifer."

When I got to Columbus, I called Shay to get her address, and the address she gave me was in the neighborhood Crystal's parents lived in. If she lived there, her bank account was very healthy. I pulled up to this house with a gate, pressed the button, and the gate swung open. I proceeded up the driveway, and as I reached the house at the top of the hill, I saw several cars. My mind started wandering as I came to a stop. I hesitated to get out, and I reached under the seat to grab my pistol.

The front doors of the house opened, and Shay stepped out in a nightgown and nothing underneath. I went inside, still clutching the handle of my 45 tight. She led me into her bedroom.

"So Shay, whose cars are those outside?"

"They are my cars. Who else's would they be?"

"I don't know. That's why I asked." I paused for a second and then asked, "So, how in the hell you get all of this shit?"

"If I tell you, then I would have to kill you," she said with a smile on her face.

"Oh, okay. Well, hey, it's not my business as long as I can stay here with you."

"Would you like to? I mean, you were a perfect gentleman to me, and I never had that, so I would love for you to stay around."

We talked, ate, laughed, and talked more, getting to know each other. Time slipped by, and I had to get to the house, so she walked me out and gave me a hug. As she wrapped her arms around me, the softness of her body was incredible. As I pulled out the subdivision, she called, and we talked until I got to the house.

"Well, beautiful, I will talk to you tomorrow."

"You promise? Because I would love to spend more time with you, Monta, if that's okay with you."

"I would love that, sweetheart! I really enjoyed our time and conversation."

"So did I. Even though I was getting out the shower when you pulled up and buzzed me, you were a perfect gentleman, and that gave me so much respect for you, Monta."

"You are more than your body and looks, Shay. You are a very, very intelligent young lady, and I learned that in a couple of hours."

"Thank you, Monta. That really means a lot, and you are outstanding yourself."

"I will call you in the a.m., beautiful. Goodnight."

I went into the house, showered, and jumped in the bed. The next morning I was awakened by the ring of my phone. It was Jennifer saying, "Hey, Monta, my doctor released me, so you don't have to come down, but you can come by the house if you want to."

"Well, I will come by when I get off or tomorrow if that's okay with you."

"That would be great."

After hanging up with Jennifer, I called to hear Shay's beautiful voice. "Hey, Monta, what you doing?"

"I'm heading to you."

"Right now?"

"Right now, so get up and get ready."

I headed over to Shay's house. She buzzed me in, and as the door swung open, she jumped in my arms, and the action started. Her robe hit the floor, and she was on my shoulders from the hall to the couch as she yelled, "Music on!" Teddy P started playing as I kissed her beautiful, soft lips. Her pussy got wet, and I moved to her perky nipples. She arched her back, and I moved down to her thighs, the prettiest thighs you would ever see. Soft and yellow.

I moved on down to her perfect juicy lips. I kissed the inside of her thigh and felt the pulse of her pussy jumping, so I introduced my tongue to her lips and with the proper introduction of *"Good morning, lips. Meet tongue."*

I gently placed my tongue on her clit, and my lips on her lips as I started a new meaning of French kiss. As I sucked on her clit, flicking my tongue, she screamed and came as she fought against me, trying to push me away. The strength of my arms overpowered the urge of her weakness.

"Monta, I can't take it," she cried. "This is too much for me. I'm about to squirt." She closed her eyes, and during the four-play, I slid my dick in as she started to squirt. She bit her lips and pulled me closer as I dropped dick deep in her walls, causing an eruption like she never felt before. She cried as I stroked her pussy nice and slow, hitting spots she didn't know existed as I sucked on her breasts, sending her into the earth's atmosphere.

As Shay's eyes closed tighter, her mouth dropped open with her sweet moans and screams. "Why do you fuck so good? Please, please tell me. I need to hear it, Monta. Why?"

"Because I mastered your body." I grinded harder, and she drove her nails into my back in response to the pressure and power of my dick as she creamed and came over and over again.

We locked eyes, and the scene became more passionate, and the movements were more personal and deep. As the heat from our bodies grew, the more sweat we created. She wrapped her legs around me, begging me not to leave, biting me softly, and making me pay more attention to her beautiful eyes and face. We reached our points as we released our emotions into each other. I felt the love in her starting to grow for me. Feeling this made me open up more because my heart melted on the first kiss. Even though she wasn't Precious, she was a blanket to my cold, broken heart.

We laid on the couch and talked until it was time for me to head to work. We got in the shower and started the second round of our show. Then, I showered and got dressed. She made me lunch, walked me to the door, and kissed me.

"Have a good day, Monta!"

"Thanks, baby. You too."

On my drive to work, my mind drifted back to Precious. I could never get rid of my thoughts of her. She had a face I couldn't seem to live without. I made it to work, and Miya texted me and said we had something to talk about. I replied, "okay," and headed in the building.

My workday went by easy. My job ran well, and around 7:00, Tip came in. I was sitting in the breakroom when my phone went off, and she asked me to come by her job to talk. So, I left out the breakroom and stopped by her job. She gave me her famous smile and said, "My period hasn't come yet, Monta, but if I'm pregnant, I'm not keeping it."

"What do you mean, if you're pregnant, you're not keeping it?"

"Just what I said!"

"Well, we are off tomorrow. I will go get you a test and bring it to you." I went back to work with my mind really spinning out of control.

Miya wanted to talk. Tip thought she was pregnant, and Jennifer just lost a baby. When it was time to hit the clock, I left to see what was going on at the house. I headed down 103 with my mind all cloudy and heart racing. My phone rang, and I heard a voice that was always so calming to my ears.

"Hey, Tina, how are you today, beautiful?"

"I'm fine, Monta. How was your day at work?"

"It went well, sweetheart. Just wish I was with you right now!"

"Awwwww, what's wrong, love?"

"Just need to be near you, sweetheart."

"Well, we need to make that possible then. Don't you think?"

"Very much so, beautiful! So, how has your day been, young lady?"

"It's been busy. I can say that much."

"Sounds like you need me, also."

"Yeah, it would be nice to feel your arms around me, comforting me at this moment. Hell, any moment with you would be great for me."

"Soon, baby. Trust me, real soon. Tina, can I call you back, baby?"

"Yes, I'm about to shower and get ready for bed anyway, so I will just text you."

I went into the house, and Miya was sitting on the couch, so I sat down beside her. She went into the bathroom and brought me a pregnancy test back that read "pregnant." At that moment, I knew there was going to be some more drama, but she was calm and excited.

The next day, I headed to LaGrange. On the way, I stopped and grabbed a test and took it to Tip. She took the test, and it was positive.

Weeks went by, and me and Shay saw each other every day. She gave me a key to the house, and I had a key to every car in the yard. One day, I was sitting at Shay's house watching TV. I got a call from Tip saying that her friend took her to get an abortion that morning. I was lost for words, so we went weeks without speaking to each other. One day, she called me up, asking if I could come to see her so we could talk. I was close by, so I stopped by, and she told me her reason for going through with the abortion. I forgave her, but I would never forget the life she took from both of us.

I left Tip's and was headed to Shay's house when I ran across a number on my phone that I needed to call months ago. I called and got no answer, but as I got on 85, she returned my call.

"Hey, how are you, beautiful?"

"Who is this?"

"So, you don't have my number saved in your phone anymore?"

"Well, I have a new phone, so I don't have any numbers saved."

"This is Monta!"

"Oh, hey, stranger. How are you?"

"I'm great, and yourself?"

"I'm doing fine, just tired."

"You just getting off work?"

"Yes, and my feet are killing me!"

"Sounds like you need me to come fix that for you then, huh?"

"That would be awesome if you could make that happen."

"So, Tenia. Are you taken?"

"No, I'm single, and yourself?"

"Well, I just got out of a situation. So can I make you mine, pretty lady?"

"If you treat me right, you can."

"I would treat you no other way, beautiful."

"Well, let's see where things go from here."

We talked until I got to the house. As I pulled in the yard, Shay was pulling up right behind me.

"Hey, baby. Where you coming from, home?"

"No, I'm coming from LaGrange."

"Oh, okay. Are you hungry?"

"Not really, but if you're hungry, I will fix you something to eat."

"That would be nice. You know I love your cooking."

"Monta, I have something to tell you."

"What's that, beautiful?"

"I'm pregnant, Monta."

I turned to look at her, and she was crying.

"What's wrong, baby?"

"Monta, I'm pregnant with your child. The guy that I was dating for the last fifteen years is a big-time drug dealer. He will be getting out in six months."

"What the fuck? So, what are you saying, Shay? All this shit is his?"

"No. This is mine, but if he sees me with a baby, he will kill me, Monta!"

"How long has he been locked up, Shay?"

"He's been gone for ten years. Out of those ten years, you are the first person I have ever messed with because of my fear of him. I moved here to get away from his family and his crew. No matter where I go, they always find me. I'm sorry for putting you in harm's way, Monta. I didn't think that I was going to fall in love with you. But that's why it didn't bother me when you said you had a woman."

"Look, Shay, you would never put me in any harm. Trust me, I don't know what you have going, but all of this should have been said from go. We could have fixed everything before it got to this point, but we are here now. So who knows that you're pregnant besides me?"

"No one. You are the first person I said anything to."

"That explains the gate and all the cameras. Now, it all makes sense. You are running from what you are afraid of. At the end of the day, you are your own person. I can't tell you how to live your life, but you have to stand up to him now. Let him know that you won't be waiting for him, and you will not be there when he gets out. Most women get hurt because they are in situations that hold onto them, so you need to shake that hold off."

"You know what, Monta? You are right. I don't need him for anything. I have my own everything, and now I have my own family," she said, calming down.

I cooked her dinner, and we watched a movie. I rubbed her feet and put her to sleep. Her phone rung later that night, and I woke her up to answer it. By no surprise, it was him, so she answered. They talked for a while until she finally got the nerve to tell him, "I think we should just cut ties at this point. I go my way, and you go yours, and by the way, I'm pregnant."

I could hear the bass in his voice as he yelled and cursed at her. I grabbed the phone and had a man to man talk with him. We got to an understanding, and he hung up.

"Monta, thank you. That's why you have my heart now because you are so amazing. I wouldn't have been able to do that alone."

"You have to understand if he is like you say he is, he will come look for you anyway, and then he would have to see me."

"Monta, he has a lot of loyal guys."

"I have West Point, sweetheart. See, we might be a small town, but we turn big wheels!"

"I love you, Monta. If you only knew how much I loved you. No matter how much I tell you or try to show you, I couldn't make you understand. You're a great man and an awesome lover, and I have you right here with me. No matter what, we will always share a bond together because I have your child in me. No matter what happens between us, this can be our secret, and you can come see us anytime you want. I don't want you to mess up your home. You are too good of a man for that."

"So, what would you like to have Shay. A girl or a boy?

"It doesn't matter to me. I'm going to love him or her to pieces!"

"And we will love you too, beautiful."

Chapter Sixteen

Tenia and I got closer as Miya and Shay both got big. Things were going great in all three places. Tenia and I set a date for her to visit. I had to work that day, but as soon as I got off, I got my things and met up with her. We got a room, put our things up, and went to grab a bite to eat. We enjoyed our dinner and headed back to the room. She showered, and I followed.

When I came out of the bathroom, I saw the beauty in her that only my heart could see because my eyes would do it no justice. This was beauty only the creator could make. I climbed in bed, and she kissed me. When her lips touched mine, I could feel her sleeping into a spell as my kisses moved further down to her love below. As my tongue gave its introduction, she couldn't hold it any longer. She let go of all her emotions as she grabbed my head and lost her mind. If those walls could talk, the things they would say.

That was the slowest lovemaking I'd ever made, and she squirted and squirted while softly calling my name. "Monta, damn, I love what you are doing to me! I have never been loved like this before. I love the way your dick fills my pussy up. Oh, shit. Monta, I'm cumming. Boy, I love the way you take your time and pay attention to every part of my body. Shit, Monta, let's cum together!"

We reached our point of no return, and I could feel the pressure from her climax and the force from her arms around me as she gripped tightly. I slow stroked her pussy until she came again and again. After our love scene, the bed was soaked, so we showered and changed the sheets. As we laid in the bed talking, she thanked me for the best loving she'd ever had.

The next morning, we went to breakfast, and Tenia asked what was on the agenda for the day.

I told her, "We're about to go load up the bikes and whip some ass."

"Really, baby?"

"Yes, we are."

"Man, I didn't bring my helmet or my jacket."

"You can wear mine, baby."

"Monta, now you know I can't wear your jacket, but I will make sure I support my man."

"I love you, beautiful, more than you would ever know."

"And I love you also, Monta! You showed me what real love felt like. You made me love you without even touching me. You saw me for who I was and loved me for who I am, not because of my pretty face or nice shape or what's between my legs. That's the kind of love I've searched for, for a long time, and who knew I had to leave Tennessee to get it? But I'm glad I did."

We picked my brother up and headed to the track. As we pulled in, the line was all the way to the road. People were everywhere. I had my brother, my baby, and my bike, and together, we were going to take over. We finally got in and unloaded the bike.

Our first victim made it hard on himself. The race was gas to gas, so we got the pot up and got in the water box. We started our burnouts at the same time. He pulled in first, and then I pulled in, and we both rolled in and turned our second bulbs on as the lights dropped. I left him sitting at the light and crossed the finish line on the back wheel.

As the day went on, we had a few more races and racked up. The night ended on a great note. We dropped my brother and the trailer off and headed back to the room. On the way back, we stopped and grabbed something to eat.

"Monta, I enjoyed our day! Watching you do something we both love to do was amazing. Baby, you were riding the hell out of that bike. You have to teach me how to do that. When I come back down, I'm bringing my jacket and helmet so you can teach me on the track."

"I would love to, baby. I know it will be fun. Watching my baby handle the fastest bike in this area would be very interesting, but I know you can handle it."

"Yeah, like I handled you last night."

"Really, Tenia. We'll see about that later on."

"How about we see about it in the shower?"

We got to the room, and she showered first. Then, I took my shower before we ate dinner. When I stepped out of the shower, she was laying on the bed with some lace boy shorts and no top. I knew at that moment what my dinner was going to be. I made my way to the bed.

She pulled me down, kissing me so soft and gentle while whispering in my ear, "Tonight, I'm taking control, so just lay back and relax."

In all my years, I had never had a woman tell me to just relax because she wanted to run the show. She was a keeper. She did her thing, and I was very impressed, but then it was my turn. I flipped her over, sliding my tongue down her body until I hit her pussy lips. Then, the show started. The motions her body made and the sounds she made were proof she reached the mountains high. She squirted and squirted, and the bed got wetter by the second. I picked her up, carried her to the couch, and bent her over, driving my dick in her steady and consistently with every stroke.

"Yes, baby! Beat that pussy just like that!" she screamed as her juices dripped all down my balls as I drove my dick deeper and deeper inside her. She looked back at me. "Yes, baby, yes! Give me that across 85 dick. Yes, daddy!"

The sound of her voice was so good to me that I couldn't hold it any longer. I released all of me in her, filling her up with love and emotions.

After our love scene, we got cleaned up, but we didn't want the night to end. She would be leaving the next day, so we stayed up and enjoyed what time we had left. The next day was hard because she had to go. We put her things in the car, and she kissed me before she drove away. I headed to West Point and got a call from Shay as I was entering town.

"Hey, baby, what you doing? And why haven't I heard from you this weekend, Monta?" Shay asked.

"I was handling some business, baby."

"Oh, okay, some business, huh? Well, I hope that business is not another woman! If it's not Miya or me that you are handling business with, then you're fucking up. I will make sure I find her, so we can beat your ass together!"

"Really, baby? I mean, you both are pregnant, so I would just run around in a circle. You can't catch me."

"Oh, believe me. I got something that will catch you! Now, hurry up and come on home, so that you can feed me and this baby."

"I will be there later on, baby. I love you."

"I love you too, Monta. Just hurry up, please. My back and feet are hurting, and it's all your fault."

I hung up from Shay and stopped by my uncle's house and hung out with him for a while. Then, I got a call from Miya telling me that her water broke, so I hurried to Columbus. As I reached the hospital, my phone was blowing up with calls from Miya saying, "Monta, you need to hurry up. This boy is not waiting."

I made it to the delivery room, and she was already prepped and ready, but our son was not trying to come until the nurse gave Miya that Pitocin. Twenty minutes later, she gave birth to a healthy baby boy. The smile on my face was everlasting. After Miya was discharged from the hospital, we moved back to West Point, and things were going great.

Shay was three weeks away from her due date, and Tenia and I were cool. As the week went by, Tenia and I made plans for me to come up and spend the weekend with her. As Friday approached, I got my things together and ready to go. At the end of my shift Thursday night, I got a call from Shay.

"Hey, baby, what are you doing?" she asked.

"Just getting off work. What you got going on, young lady?"

"I was just thinking about you. I need some dick, so this baby can come out of me."

"Well, I have to go to the house and shower first, baby. You know I hate to feel dirty."

"Monta, get your ass down here and get here now! I want some dick, and I'm not waiting. I will give you a bath when you get here."

I headed to Columbus, and as I get off 103, Tenia called. "Hey, Monta, what you doing?"

"Nothing much, baby. Heading to Columbus. What you doing up this time of night?"

"I couldn't sleep. Up thinking about tomorrow and the things we will do when you get here."

"Well, all we have now is a wake-up, and I will be on my way."

"I know, baby, and I'm so excited and so ready to see you, Monta."

"What you going to do when you see me?"

"It's going to be a big surprise."

"Well, you can tell me, and I will still act surprised, baby."

"No, you will see tomorrow, so stop asking."

"Baby, so you doing me like that. You know I would tell you!"

"Monta, you will know tomorrow."

"Okay, I love you and goodnight. If I stay on the phone with you, I will keep asking, so I'm going to sleep," I said and ended the call as I pulled up to Shay's gate and put the code in. The gate swung open, and I started up the hill. The front doors were open. Shay and all her belly stood there in heels and a pink lace nightgown with nothing under it but her beautiful yellow skin and those long bowlegs.

As I reached the house, she waved for me to come in. I stepped in the door and saw that she had rose petals laid out from the door to the shower. She took my clothes off, throwing them all over before we stepped into the shower. The water steamed the glass as she washed my body. She pushed me against the wall and dropped down to her knees and sucked my dick deep in her throat, sucking until she pulled the first nut out of me. She made my knees so weak that I almost hit the floor. I wanted to take the show into the bedroom, but she stopped me. She turned around and grabbed the shower handle and said, "Now, fuck me until my water breaks."

I slid my dick in slowly, and my strokes started long and deep. As she screamed, I went deeper and stronger until she couldn't take anymore. As she exploded, I finished my shower, ate dinner, and put her to bed before I headed out. I didn't want to go, but I had to, so I locked up and headed out the door. As I made my way back to West Point, I called up Tina to check on her.

"Hey, beautiful. How are you?"

"Hey, Monta. I was just thinking about you. How has your day been, handsome?"

"Well, it's been great, beautiful. Just ready to get to you."

"You need to stop playing and make that happen."

"I'm working on it, baby. Trust me. I will call you tomorrow. I was just calling to check on you, sweetheart."

"Oh, okay. Well, I love you. Goodnight, Monta."

"Goodnight, beautiful."

As I pulled up to the house, I just sat there with the woman I really wanted on my mind. Through the sea of women I was dealing with, all I could see in my head was Precious. As the years passed, I thought about her more. Out of all the girls I dated, she was the youngest but the only one who kept my attention. I couldn't sleep some nights because every time I closed my eyes, her smile played repeatedly in my mind. The beauty of her smile still reflected through my eyes. I didn't know what to do or how to do it, but I needed to find a way back into her heart and vision.

After my moment, I went inside, and sitting on the couch waiting on me were Miya and a crying baby. I sat down beside her, and we talked as she rocked him back to sleep. I picked my son up and laid him in his crib as she made her way into the bedroom.

"Monta, where have you been?" she asked as soon as I stepped into our bedroom.

"I worked over, baby. I'm sorry I didn't call you and tell you. I just got caught up in my work if you know what I mean."

"Why do you smell like soap and a woman then, Monta? Who have you been fucking? You must think I'm stupid or something, Monta?"

"No, baby. I know you're not stupid, sweetheart. I would never try to play you like that, so please don't think that. Your pussy is the only pussy this dick is attracted to Miya."

"It better be, or I'm going to cut it off."

"If you cut it off, then you can't get any. I mean, it's not like you get it anyway. I have to fight you to get the little bit that I do get."

"Okay, Monta. Goodnight," she said, waving me off.

"See, that's my point. The truth hurts, don't it?" I said before I jumped in the shower.

My mind went back to the scene me and Shay created. She wasn't Precious, but I could see my life unfolding with her. I finished up in the shower and got dressed. My mind was still playing the show that me and Shay put on as I laid down and closed my eyes.

The next morning was a great start to an amazing day. I called out of work, so I could surprise Tenia with my early arrival. I headed to Tennessee, and as my drive and music started to sink in, my phone rang. On the other end was a voice I didn't expect to hear from.

"Hey, Tip, how are you?"

"I'm fine, and yourself?"

"I'm doing great, driving."

"Monta, can you do me a favor?"

"If it has anything to do with me coming somewhere, I can't. I'm headed to Tennessee."

"Oh, okay. Well, you can't help. So what are you going up there for?"

"I have to handle some business."

"So you're going to fuck some bitch, huh?"

"I don't fuck with bitches. Thank you."

I hung up with Tip as I pull up at Tenia's house. Her car was gone, so I knocked on the door. Her sister-in-law let me in. I texted Tenia and told her that I wouldn't be able to make it up this weekend. I knew that would break her heart and mess up her plans. She called me, but I didn't answer.

A few minutes later, she pulled up and saw my truck sitting in the yard. She ran into the house and jumped into my arms as we laughed together. Tenia got dressed, and we took a ride through the city. Our destination was a beautiful view that overlooked the city of Nashville. We got out the car and were climbing the hill when she grabbed my hand and looked into my eyes. She dropped down on her knees, still gazing into my eyes, and said the sweetest words any man could only ever dream of a woman saying to him.

"Monta, you are everything any woman could ever ask and pray for. And you belong to me. You gave me love like no man has ever given me. I fell in love with you just the way you said I would. You loved me for who I was and not my beautiful face or what you could get from me, but me. And out of all that, I would love to ask you would you do me the honor of being my husband?"

"Yes, I would, baby!"

"Monta, you make me so happy."

We headed over to the park, where she did a photoshoot and walked over to the picnic table and talked and laughed like we always did. Then, Tenia switched everything up when she pulled my dick out and slid down on it as she sat on my lap. The warmth of her pussy felt so good to me as she rolled her hips, grinding on my dick. I pulled her down even closer gripping her beautiful breasts as she made love to my dick as the night air breezed through our bodies like the waves of the sea. Once our love was made, we headed to the house for part two of our celebration.

We went into our cocoon of passion, and I laid her down on the bed and played tunes on her pussy lips as she moaned and shook from the pressure of my tongue. My thoughts and mind played that scene over and over again. I could see her fall to her knees as my tongue ran deeper and deeper inside her pussy walls. She pushed me away as she squirted and screamed. As she pulled me closer again, I slipped my dick in her valley of love, stroking and grinding to the sounds of Jagged Edge, and going deeper to every beat. The way her pussy lips squeezed the head of my dick was the beginning of the production of a baby. My strokes got stronger and stronger, and she cried softly in my ears.

"Yes, Monta. Go deeper, baby. Damn, Monta, I'm about to cum. Please, cum with me." As the words rolled off her lips, we both exploded!

After we cleaned up, we laid in bed, planning the greatest wedding ever. The next day, we roamed the town, enjoying our time and the proposal that was blessed by the night stars of Nashville. Tenia wasn't Precious, but the bond we shared would forever be strong, whether we were together or not. We grabbed something to eat and headed back to the house where we ate and shared memories that were touching to the both of us. As her tears started falling, I became the shoulder that she deserved.

We got ready for bed and lay down, but before we closed our eyes, I had to draw another painting on her sexy body and send her to space with the tender kisses and the magic of my tongue and lips followed by the force of my dick. We ended our session with her in my arms. We slept until the sun woke us up. I rolled over and kissed her, knowing it was time for me to hit the road. I didn't want to leave ever, but I knew I had to go.

I showered, got dressed, and hit the road. Tenia called, and we talked until it was time for her to go to work. The sad 'talk to you later' hit us again. I reached West Point a short while later, and my phone rang. It was Shay telling me she was going into labor, so I rushed to Columbus.

As I arrived at the hospital, Shay was ready to push so I rushed up to labor and delivery. I walked into her room and grabbed her hand as she began pushing. Fifteen minutes later, our beautiful baby girl was here. When I looked into her eyes, I saw Brea all over again. I held her and tears fell down my face. Looking at her and her mom was the start of me changing my ways.

As the weeks went by, I spent a lot of time with Shay. Me and Tenia didn't talk as much, and I had my eyes on a young lady at work. I was rolling by on my lift one Friday morning when this particular young lady walked by. I honked my horn at her, and she stopped. I jumped down off my lift and asked her name.

She said, "Mookie, and what's yours?"

"Hey, Mookie. I'm Monta!" I held a conversation with her, getting her attention. "Are you taken?"

"For now I am," she replied, and I knew that wouldn't last long after I struck up a conversation with her. I let a week go by before I smiled at her, and the moment she saw that smile, I had her. We exchanged numbers and started hanging out, getting to know each other until one day she texted me and said she was horny.

Me: Sweetheart, I don't think you can handle me.

Mookie: Boy, I can handle anything you throw at me.

Me: Are you sure?

Mookie: I'm positive!

We set up a date for later that night, and when I got off, I hurried to the house where I showered, got dressed, and headed to pick her up. We went to Applebee's and ate and shared stories. After we finished our dinner, we went next door and got a room.

I turned the TV on and hit the lights. By the time I turned around, she was lying in bed without a stitch of clothes. So in my head, I knew she was saying to herself 'I'm about to fuck the shit out of this little ass man!' But that wouldn't be the case, so I climbed in bed ready to prove her wrong.

She started kissing me and pulled me closer, saying, "Let's get this over with." So I kissed her back, and the first touch of my lips let her know I didn't come to play any games.

My kisses traced her slim, sexy body, and she moaned and shivered from the touch of my lips. I went deeper into her valley as I introduced my tongue to her clit. She grabbed my head and lost her mind. I was just giving her the introduction just to get her pussy wet enough to ease the pain, so I stuck the head in the entrance of her lips and felt the tightness of her pussy. Then, I proceeded to slide it in, and it wouldn't go. I tried and tried again, and we still didn't have any luck.

"Monta, it's not going to fit!"

"Yes, it is."

I went back down and painted a portrait on her canvas. The touch of my lips and tongue made her body lose control as she cried and moaned. As she came, I eased on up and forced my dick in Mookie's tight pussy, stroking and grinding as she cried and cried in my ear.

"Monta, I can't take anymore, baby. Your dick is too big for my pussy. Please, hurry up and cum."

My stroke went deeper, and I could see the tears rolling down Mookie's face. The way she moaned and called my name made me go into a mode she wasn't ready for. The longer I stroked, the bigger my dick got. The tightness of her lips let me know she was about to feel pain like she had never felt before, but this was our first session. I couldn't let her feel all of my tricks.

She bit her lips and closed her eyes as she released all of her emotions, and I was at the point of no return as I exploded, feeling the heat from my climax. She looked at me with a surprised expression on her face. She thought she was going back to work to brag about fucking the hell out of me, but things didn't go her way.

We got cleaned up and headed out. The ride was silent, and the expression on her face spoke all the words that she was thinking. I dropped her off and headed down the road.

On my way home, I called Shay to check on her and our daughter, but she didn't answer. I called again and still got no answer. My mind started running, wondering if she was okay. As I got off the West Point exit, my phone went off, and it was her.

"Baby, why didn't you answer the phone?"

"I was fixing your daughter something to eat, baby. I'm sorry I didn't have my phone with me."

"I'm coming to spend the weekend with you guys to give you a break. Okay, sweetheart?"

"We would love that, Monta! You don't know how long I stay up at night thinking about you and the things we could have together."

"I know, baby, but you know my situation. You have given me things that I can't take back, love that I will never forget, and smiles that money can't buy. Trust me, I understand where you are coming from."

"Well, I love you, Monta, and I will talk to you tomorrow."

"I love you also, beautiful. Please don't ever forget it."

I made it to the house, and my mind started running with thoughts about life with Shay and the joy it would bring. I could touch her without any problems, make love to her, and create the stars. My life would be a lot better off with Shay, but I just couldn't leave Miya even though my mind, heart, and soul were telling me to.

I walked into the house, took a shower, and texted Tina.

Me: Hey, beautiful. What you doing?

Tina: Nothing much. I was just thinking about you and when I would be able to see you.

Me: Well let's plan for next weekend if that's ok with you.

Tina: That would be awesome. I will come your way if you want me to!

Me: That's great because we have a race that weekend.

Tina: I would love to see that. Damn I can't wait to see you! All I been thinking about is that kiss you gave me that night at the store.

Me: If you thought that kiss was something wait until you get this TD!

Tina: What is a TD?

Me: This tongue and dick action. I mean, I'm not bragging. I'm just warning you, that's all.

Tina: Well, I'm starting the countdown right now. I'm ready to spend this weekend in your arms.

Me: I'm ready to be next to you, beautiful. I will call you tomorrow ok.

The next day, I packed a bag and headed to Columbus to spend the weekend with the woman I should've been with and our daughter. As I pulled to the gate, my eyes filled with tears.

All of these years, I had been searching for someone who had no interest in me anymore. On that journey, I'd hurt a lot of great women, but something had to change and soon. I was with a person I really didn't want or need to be with and had a beautiful lady in the house who deserved me, but I couldn't seem to shake Miya. All that I could do was hope that Shay felt the same way I did.

The gates opened, and I started up the hill. My queen and princess were standing in the doorway waiting on me. The joy I had when I saw the smiles on their faces was like no other greater feeling a man could have and wish for.

Our weekend was outstanding and moved fast. As the time drew near the end of it, my heart started crying. This was my home. This was where I wanted to be and who I wanted and needed to be with, but I got my things ready to go and moved slowly as I kissed my ladies goodbye and walked out the door. I was making a mistake that I needed to right, but it wasn't the time.

As I got on 185, Mookie called and asked what I was doing.

"Nothing much. Just driving headed home."

"Don't you want to come to see me? I want some dick."

"Well, it will be late when I get back, but I will make sure you get some tomorrow."

"You promise?"

"Yes, baby. I promise. What you doing, young lady?"

"Just finished a photoshoot and thinking about you."

"Well, I will talk to you tomorrow, okay, beautiful?"

The next day we got together and made music. She fell in love with the way I paid attention to her body and mind. We created a special bond very quickly and spent time together over the next week, but that weekend belonged to Tina. So when Friday came, I hit the clock and called Tina to see how far she'd made it.

"Hey, baby. How close are you?"

"I'm going through Mississippi."

"Oh, okay. Drive careful. I love you."

"I love you too, Monta!"

I was in the room, waiting for her to pull up. At 5:30 a.m., she called and told me she was outside. I ran downstairs, grabbed her things, and brought her to the room. She took a shower, and when she stepped out, my eyes were stunned, and my mind was blown. Out of all the women I had over the years, she was the sexiest, and she had them all by ten to twelve years. She dried off and walked up to me, and the show started.

I picked her up on my shoulder and slid her down on my tongue, drawing a perfect picture. Her body moved in ways I was sure she never knew existed. I laid her on the bed and sucked on her clit so gently as I slid one finger in her pussy and the other in her ass. She exploded. Her body lost control as she shook and screamed from the love my tongue was making to her clit.

She squirted and screamed as she cried out to me, "Monta, I can't feel my body, but this is the best feeling in the world!"

At that moment, I knew her soul had left her body. I climbed up her body and slid my dick in so slowly and gently that the width and length of my dick was too much for her. Still, she took it like no one had ever before. My strokes went deep and on beat, and she scratched my back as I went deeper.

Moaning and shaking, she said, "Damn, Monta. It's everything you said it would be and more. I can't take it anymore, Monta! What you doing to me?"

"I'm giving you what you never had before, making love to you like you never imagined."

"And it feels so good and hurts at the same time, baby. Damn, Monta, I'm about to cum!" As she came, I went deeper and exploded all inside of her, knowing that she couldn't get pregnant, and for the first time, it didn't matter.

We cleaned up and laid down to sleep. A few hours later, I was up and out the door. I left her asleep. She was tired from her long drive, and I wanted her to rest while I headed up the road to pick up my bike. By the time I got to Toney's house, he was just finishing up. We loaded the bike, and I headed back down the road. As I got back to the room, Tina was up waiting for me.

"Hey, baby, did you get enough sleep?" I asked.

"Yes, I did. That was the best sleep ever. No kids running around screaming and waking me up."

"Are you ready to go to the track?"

"Yes, I'm ready. I've been waiting on you."

We headed to my brother's house. I stopped and grabbed her something to drink and a bite to eat. My brother and his wife were sitting on the porch when we pulled up. I greeted my brother with, "Cat Daddy, what's up, bruh?"

"Nothing. Waiting on your slow ass. Do you have enough nitrous?"

"Probably not."

"Well, you better go back there and fill your bottle up then," he said.

I took my bottle off the bike and filled it, knowing I wouldn't need it. We left for the track, and when we arrived, the crowd was already there. We went through the gates and down the hill to find a spot to park. We set everything up, and I took time to sit down and talk to Tina before taking the bike off the trailer.

I finally unloaded my bike and made a pass. My brother got a race up, motor to motor, so we got to the line and did our burnouts and staged. He lit both of his bulbs, and I slowly rolled in mine. As the lights dropped, I took off. The front-wheel picked up around the 330 and across the finish line I went. As I rolled back around, I parked and sat with Tina while Toney worked on my bike.

The day was great. My bike ran good, and at the end of the night, Toney got up another race, but they backed out. I wanted to spray my bike for the first time since the new build, so Toney turned the gas on as I rolled to the starting line. I staged and flipped my nitrous switch on and rolled into my second bulb. The light dropped, and everything got quiet as I twisted the throttle. The bike spun and wheelied then spun again. The nitrous came in so hard that the bike spat, caught on fire, and shut off. I rolled to the return lane, both heartbroken about the fire and happy that the fire went out.

Toney came down and pushed me back to the trailer. I loaded the bike up and hung out with Tina until it was time for us to leave.

"Baby, you were riding that bike. You scared me, but you rode it. I see that you can handle more than your dick."

We laughed and headed out. I dropped my brother and the bike off and headed back to the room with Tina. We showered, ate, and laid in bed for a while, watching TV. She started kissing me and rubbing my dick as I kissed her back. Her body got weak, and I took control of the session, giving her the feeling that she'd wanted all day. When we finished, she laid in my arms and closed her eyes.

The next morning, we woke up to the sad thought of her leaving. We both got dressed, and I put her things in the car, kissed her, and said goodbye. I headed home, and the thought of going through those doors made me sick to my stomach. I ended up taking a shower, getting dressed, and heading to Columbus to see Shay and my daughter. Shay was sitting by the pool playing with our princess when I arrived.

"Hey, beautiful. What are you two doing?"

"Nothing much. Just sitting here trying to figure out what we want to eat."

"How about you let me take you guys out to eat?"

"That would be nice. I'm tired of sitting at the house anyway, so let's go now!"

We jumped in the Range and headed to Atlanta. The feeling I got when I was with this part of my family was great.

"So, what would you like to eat, beautiful?" I asked.

"I really had a taste for some Cheesecake Factory."

"Well, that's where we are headed then, my love. As you wish."

"Monta, you are such a great man. Why couldn't I have met you sooner?"

"That's the same thing I ask myself every night," I admitted.

We ate, went shopping, took family portraits, and enjoyed our time together as a family before heading home. Shay asked if I would marry her, and even though I wanted to, I couldn't sell her a dream.

I just said, "If things were different, we would already be married."

We made it back to the house, and I made sure they made it inside safely. I locked up and set the alarm, then I headed home. Miya wasn't happy about me being away from home all the time, but I couldn't bring myself to be there for her like that.

The next day, I went to work. Mookie and I were on bad terms because she found out about my relationship with Miya. In the meantime, I met a beautiful young lady by the name of Grace. Her smile and looks went with her name. Her walk was fantastic, and the way she called my name brought chills to my body. We started hanging out and getting to know each other better.

One night, I took Grace to the movies and out to eat, and we headed back to her place. The moment we stepped through the door, Grace jumped on me, kissing me, snatching off clothes, and knocking over things as if we were having a knockdown, drag-out. I took control of the situation and slowed things down. She was younger than me and didn't quite know what she wanted, so I gave her a dose of what she really needed.

I laid Grace down, kissing every inch of her body and sending her mind into space while I controlled her body. I sucked her beautiful, perfect breasts, and made my way down her curves, reaching the falls to her juices. My tongue performed CPR on her clit. She went into shock, shivering and shaking, squirting and fighting me off as she came and came. As I made my way up her body, I slid my dick in her tight, wet pussy, stretching her lips to the max. She screamed and sank her nails into my back, crying, "Please, go slow."

I stroked deep, in and out to the sounds of Pleasure P. The deeper I went, the louder she screamed, "Monta, I can't handle it, but you're doing something strange to me, and it feels so damn good. Baby, go slower!"

Grace wet the bed as we created the greatest masterpiece. The night went on, and the mood got deeper. The intensity heightened when she squeezed me and exploded right before I did. That climax was the greatest pressure I had released in a long time. At that moment, we both knew she was pregnant.

Days went by, and we got closer, but I knew that I couldn't bring her heart too deep into my life. I eased up and drew away slowly. Weeks later, I had changed jobs. Grace and I were still doing great, but not as great as she wanted us to be.

One day, on my new job, I spoke to this young lady, and she turned her nose up at me. My little cousin yelled, "Cuz, that's a stuck up ass bitch right there. You can't pull her."

"I mean, not that I want her. I'm just a nice person," I responded.

"Cuz, I bet you fifty dollars you can't pull that one!"

"I'm not going to make a stupid bet like that. Come on, man. That's a lady, not a game."

"So, you scared because you know you can't do it, right? I tell you what. I will bet five hundred to your two hundred."

"Okay, bet."

All week, I didn't even look her way as she made her rounds. The following Monday, she walked by, and I smiled and waved. She waved back. I let a few more days go by, and I noticed she would look over to see if she could see me. Now, it was time to make my move. I caught her coming from lunch, and as I walked by, I grabbed her attention.

"Hey, beautiful. How are you?"

"I'm fine. My name is Trina, but thanks for the compliment."

"You know, it's more where that came from."

"Oh, really? Why would I need more?"

"Because you deserve it. I mean, I watch you all day, every day, walk up through here with a frown on your face. Why don't you smile?"

"I'm at work. What is there to smile about?"

"I feel you there. So, Trina, are you taken?"

"Should I be? You must be the one that wants to take me?"

"Maybe or maybe not. You would have to give me your number so we could find out."

"You did that so smooth that I'm going to give it to you. Let's see what you do with it."

I took the number and held it for a few days before I called. The weekend came, and I was bored and didn't have anything to do, so I decided to call Trina and ask her out on a date.

"Hello, who is this?"

"It's me, beautiful—Monta!"

"Hey, how are you? I was wondering when I was going to hear from you."

"What you doing? Would you like to go out?"

"I would love to."

"Well, send me your address, and I will pick you up in an hour." I hung up and got dressed, then headed her way.

When I arrived at her house, my mind told me to treat her as if she was the perfect mate for me. I knocked on her door, and she opened the door with a smile.

"Wow, you look nice, and I love a woman in heels."

"Well, thank you, and you are looking and smelling nice yourself!"

"I put on my best for a beautiful queen like yourself."

"You must be trying to get in my drawers or something?"

"No, ma'am. Why would you say that?"

"I'm just messing with you, but I know that you want to."

"You're not ready for me, young lady."

"If you say so, and I'm a grown-ass woman, sweetheart," she pointed out.

We pulled up at LongHorn Steakhouse. I opened her door, and we went inside. As we sat down to eat, I noticed one of my exes sitting a few seats back, so I really put on a show then. The waitress took our order, and we laughed and enjoyed each other. We finished our dinner and headed to the movies. The movie was great, and the time we spent was great.

Over the next few weeks, we talked and hung out. Work was different for us. She came to break when I went on break, and we talked and laughed like we were the only ones in the building.

We were pretty much great friends until she called me one night to come over. When I showed up, things went fast, and we found ourselves between the sheets making music as the room heated up. Her body obeyed my commands as the night went on, and our session eventually ended. I found myself somewhere I wasn't expecting to be, and as time passed me and Trina kicked it and kept making music until I put all my focus in Shay and our family. We'd had fun while it lasted, but my family was more important. I slowed down a little and focused on the two women who mattered the most.

One day, I received phone calls from Trina and Grace, telling me they were pregnant. The thoughts that went through my head wouldn't stop coming. I didn't know how I was going to break this news to either one of them and not break their hearts. I kept it to myself and moved on with life. But no matter what I did or where I went Precious would always come back and lay on my heart and mind. It was time for me to try something different, so I looked for a better and different job.

Chapter Seventeen

I started at Caterpillar Things, and I was loving my job. Me and Shay were still cool, and Miya was becoming more of what I wanted.

Just when I thought things were going great, I met this beautiful young lady named Kia. She was cool, laid back, and was falling for me. We hung out a lot and got to know each other better, and in the midst of that, Mookie wanted back in.

She called me, saying, "Monta, I miss you and the love we used to make. You understood me and appreciated me for who I was. I wish you would see things the way I see them or at least let me get some dick."

Kia and I kicked it for a while, made music, and enjoyed doing it until she found out about Miya. We still saw each other from time to time but not as much as we used to, but me and Mookie got things back the way they used to be. Whenever I wanted her, all I had to do was call, and whenever she wanted me, she would call or text. We could have fun doing anything. If we were making love, she would make me laugh. The bond we had was unbreakable.

However, I got tired of the different women and only wanted one woman, and that woman I couldn't get close to for some reason. She would speak every now and then, but she wouldn't let me in. The love we once had was dead in her eyes, but to me our love was forever.

One day, I was heading to lunch, and I made a pit stop at Raceway and ran into the prettiest woman I had ever seen.

"Hey, beautiful. How are you?"

"Fine, and you?"

"I was rushing to get me something on my lunch break and saw you. Now, I'm no longer hungry anymore. So, beautiful, are you taken?"

"No, sir. I'm single, but are you taken?"

"Yes, I am, but I would love to get to know you if that's not a problem with you. So, ma'am, what's your name?"

"My name is Shuntae, and yours?"

"I'm Monta. You see, we would go great together, Monta and Shuntae. Now, don't that just sound great as one?"

"If you say so."

"I know so! Look, I have to head back to work, so let me see your phone, so I can store my number for you." She handed me her phone, and I entered my number and gave it back to her. "Make sure you use it, beautiful!"

"I will, handsome."

I headed back to work. My phone rang, and on the other end, I heard the sweet little voice that I'd just left say, "Hey, Monta. I was just making sure you gave me the right number, that's all. I will call you later on, or you can just text me if you like."

For the rest of the night, we texted back and forth, getting to know each other better. She made the rest of my shift go by smoothly. When it was time to get off, I hit the clock, and Kia called and asked me to bring her something to eat. I hurried home, showered, and headed her way.

As I headed down 29, I stopped off and grabbed Kia a bite to eat and made my way to her house. She stepped outside, and my heart dropped. She looked like a doll. Everything was perfect. Her hair laid to the side, and her lips were juicy and shining. She wore a t-shirt and boy shorts, and from the looks of her beauty, my night couldn't get any better.

Kia kissed me, and things went south, from her lips to her breasts. I moved slowly and gently as I made my way to the lips of the valley and put an arch in her back with every flick of my tongue. I slid my fingers in places that made her moan and scream. I painted a portrait of a beautiful swan as the session moved on. The room spun to the strokes of my tongue, making her cum over and over again. I rose to the top and slipped my dick into her juicy, wet pussy. She inhaled from the pressure of my entry and scratched my back. I stroked and grinded as we fell into the sinkhole of passion, making what I knew was the best music she'd ever heard.

After our session ended, I cleaned up and headed home. As I got to the house, I got a call from Grace.

"Hey, Monta. What you doing?"

"Nothing much, baby. Just getting home."

"So, when are you coming to see me and your son?"

"I will be up there this weekend, beautiful."

"You promise?"

"I promise. What are you doing up this late?"

"I couldn't sleep for thinking about you."

"Well, I will spend the weekend with you guys. Okay, beautiful?"

"Okay."

I went inside the house, showered, and watched TV a while before laying down. Like always, when I sat still for too long, my thoughts fell into the lap of Precious. I wished that she was the one I was going home to at night, not Miya, but I had to play the cards I was dealt for a while.

That weekend, my shift ended, and I rushed home, got dressed, and headed out the door to go to Union City. An 18-wheeler passed by me, and I thought about how that was what I wanted to do instead of being in a plant. I would rather be to myself traveling the country and getting paid for it.

I got to the house, talked with Grace, and let her know what I wanted to do. With an okay from her, it was time to make a new career, not only for me but for my kids and to keep me away from all these different women.

Our weekend went great. Grace cooked for me and pampered me the entire weekend. My water was run just how I liked it. My kisses were just how I wanted them, and our nights were something I would never forget. But when the weekend was over, it was time to make my move home.

I got back and sat Miya down, and I told her what I wanted to do and what needed to be done. Without a doubt, she was on board.

I worked at Caterpillar for a couple more weeks. I got everything lined up with trucking school and all the bills figured out and handled. My first day of school went well. As the weeks went by, the road to getting my CDL was getting closer. I had driven before, so that wasn't a problem. The day came for us to take the road test, and we all waited patiently for our turns.

As I sat there waiting, I thought about the times me and Precious had and the fun and love we shared. My thoughts were so deep that I didn't hear the instructor calling my name. I hopped up and got into the truck, did the backing and parking tests, and passed that with ease.

Now, it was time for the road test. As we headed out the gate, I struck up a football conversation with the instructor to put him at ease and to make my test shorter. We headed down the road and back with no problem. When we all finished, I headed to the house to pack my things to start my new journey.

Weeks went by, and I was getting along great with my trainer, enjoying the road and the country setting. I saw different things and places, and it was amazing! I got down to my last day with my trainer. Soon, I would be in my own truck to have the space that a trucker needs. My trainer took me back to the terminal, and I was issued my truck. They checked and serviced my truck, and I checked off my items, fueled up, and headed home.

The two days I was home, I spent with my kids and fixed my truck up the way I wanted it. The day before I had to leave out, I went to Columbus and saw Shay. She wasn't happy with the decision I made.

"Monta, why do you have to go on the road? I can understand you wanting to be a truck driver, but do you have to be on the road?"

"Baby, it's only going to be a short while. I need to get the experience that I need, so I can drive local."

"But you don't have to work at all. I told you that I would take care of you and everything that needed to be taken care of."

"I know, baby, but I'm not that guy. I can't just sit there and let anybody do the things for me that I need to do. Just be patient, beautiful. I will be home as much as I need to and check on you guys, okay? I will talk to you every day, so you can hear my voice."

"Monta, I love you, and I don't ever want to lose you. I know you are with her, but I am a big part of your life also. Just remember that," Shay said before I headed out.

My first load was headed to South Carolina. The load and drop went well, and I got my next load and headed to Texas. I called Tina, letting her know that I was headed her way. As I rolled into the truck stop in Houston, she was waiting on me. I parked and went inside to take a shower. I grabbed us something to eat, and we headed back to the truck. I put a movie on, and we talked, ate, and caught up on things.

Once we finished eating, I put the playlist on that we created called "Texas Heat," and the truck saw some things that weren't viewed by many. The bed rocked to the painting on her canvas.

"Shit, Monta, I missed this dick of yours, and that tongue has gotten more intense and strong. Yes, baby, I'm about to cum!" she yelled. "Damn, that shit feels so good, Monta. Please, don't leave me!"

"Baby, I have to go, but I will be back this way. Please, believe me."

The next morning, I headed out to drop my load. My next load was headed to Dallas where my son and his mom lived, so I called Crystal and told her I was on my way to a truck stop near her.

As traffic moved slowly, I looked down, and my eyes and mind were playing tricks on me. For thirty seconds, I could have sworn I saw Precious riding next to me, smiling, but it was just me missing her smile.

As I reached the pilot, I called Crystal and told her I made it.

"I'm standing right behind you, Monta, but I can't move because I can't believe it's you! I can't believe that you are here in front of me."

"Well, it's me, baby. Everything that you left. Where is my son?"

"He's in school. Do you want to go with me to pick him up?"

"I wish I could, but I have to take this load and drop it off at Walmart, and then go to Arkansas to pick up my next load. But if it takes them a while to unload it, then I can come back here for the night."

"I really hope it takes a long time."

"I will see you later, hopefully. I love you, Crystal, and tell my baby that I love him too."

I headed over to Walmart, and trucks were lined up outside the gate, so I knew I would be here for a while. I called Crystal and told her I would be back when I got unloaded that night. Hours later, I was still waiting, and the guard called my phone and told me to pull into door nineteen. Twenty minutes later, I was unloaded with an hour on my clock. I got my paperwork and headed back to the truck stop. I found a parking spot and headed inside to shower.

I called Crystal and told her to come to pick me up. When I got out the shower and headed to my truck, she was pulling up. To see my son in person for the first time in ten years made my heart cry, and my eyes followed. That night, we spent a lot of time talking and enjoying each other. Looking at Del was like looking at Quez and Kiyon all over again.

"Monta, he has asked about you and his siblings for so long. I tell him everything about what happened and how we got here. He has so much respect and love for you. Every time a guy has tried to talk to me, he would always say 'if you don't leave my mom alone I'm going to tell my daddy.'"

"Crystal, why don't you move back? I think he would love it there."

"I've been thinking about it because it's just so much that goes on here, and I don't want him around all this mess."

For the rest of the night, we talked and laughed and just enjoyed the little time we had. I didn't want sex. I just wanted time with the two of them. The next morning, she took me back to my truck, and I headed out. When I made it to Arkansas, Crystal called me.

"Baby, we are moving back to Columbus."

"That's great. I will get to see more of you guys, and maybe we can work on what we lost," I replied thoughtfully.

I picked up my load going to Oregon and moved about the highway, watching my movies and listening to the tunes of my playlist. All I could do was think about Precious and hope one day that she would take me back. I made it to my drop, and as I was unhooking my trailer my phone rang.

"Hello, Monta. What you doing?"

"Hey, Mookie. I'm dropping my load in Oregon, about to freeze my ass off up here! How are you?"

"I'm good. When are you coming home? I miss you and your great loving. I lay in bed at night beside my husband thinking of you. I don't even allow him to touch me because he's not you. I'm tired of kidding myself like he can be everything that you were."

"I will be home next weekend. Maybe we can get together if he lets you out the house."

"When you get here, let me know, and I can meet you somewhere."

"Okay, I will do that, beautiful."

"Hey, Monta. I love you and, no matter what, please don't ever forget it. It's just something about you that sets you aside from any other man, and that makes you special to any woman, especially me."

"I love you too, baby. You are a great part of my smile." I ended the call and headed to my next pick up where I met a very unique and beautiful young lady.

"Hey, beautiful! How are you, and what's your name?"

"I'm doing great, handsome. My name is Sherry. What's yours?"

"It's nice to meet you, Sherry. I'm Monta, and it's nice to meet you. So are you taken, or do you have a friend?"

"No, I'm single at the moment."

"Well, that's a problem. Your time and kisses should be occupied by me, so let's fix that."

"Wow, I like that. I see you have a hell of a spit game."

"So, Sherry, where you from?"

"I'm from New Jersey, but I live in Delaware."

"Well, I'm from Georgia, but I would love to get to know you better. I mean, it's nothing for me to get a load to you."

"I would love that! So when can we make this happen?"

"I will be home next weekend, but when I leave back out, I will get a load to you."

"That sounds like a plan!"

"Well, make sure you keep in touch."

That week, I finished all my loads out west and headed back to Georgia. On my way home, I stopped in Hogansville and met Mookie. I pulled into the truck stop and parked then hurried in to get a shower and something to drink. I ran into a beautiful, humble young lady there.

"Hello, beautiful. How are you?"

"I'm fine. Thank you!"

"So, what's your name, sweetheart?"

"It's Kataandra, and yours?"

"Well, hello, Kataandra. I'm Monta, and it's nice to meet you. So, beautiful, are you taken?"

"No, not at the moment."

"Can I get to know you?"

"Maybe. We will have to see."

"Well, here is my number if you change your mind."

"Here is mine also. Just give me a call, and we can talk about you taking me out."

I took her number and walked back to my truck. My phone rang, and it was Mookie. "Baby, I'm here. I'm parked on the side."

"I'm coming. I just walked out the door."

I met Mookie, and we walked back to my truck, where we talked for a while before the music began to play. Kisses rolled down her body, and she begged me not to be so rough. My tongue took control of the situation, and as her hand caressed my ears, I made love to her pussy lips with my tongue while her body lost control. Her legs shook and shook. The love we made was a piece of art that was created through body chemistry and mind understanding.

As we played each scene with pure passion, she cried out, "That's why I love you so much."

The show continued, and I eased my dick in so slow and gently as she exhaled from the pain of my dick stretching her walls to the max. Her soft cry in my ears made my strokes more forceful and slow as she came and came. Her body shook and shivered from me painting on her canvas. As we came to the end of our lovely scene, we both found our peak and released our emotions together. After hours of great, sweaty lovemaking, we just laid there and talked as she curled up in my arms, not wanting to leave.

My clock was almost out, and I had to get to the house, so I walked her back to her car and headed home. I called Miya as I got off the exit and told her to come pick me up from my uncle's house. While I waited on her, I got my things together. As I was cleaning, my mind wandered away with thoughts of Precious. I packed the last of my stuff as Miya pulled up. I locked up, and we headed home. Although I'd been gone for weeks, Miya's attention, as always, wasn't on me. It never was.

At home, I washed my clothes and packed my bags. Then, I took my shower and laid down. The next morning, I got up and headed to Columbus to see Shay and my baby. As I pulled to the gate, it opened, and I pulled up the hill. She ran and jumped into my arms with kisses and tears. Behind her was my beautiful princess.

"Daddy, you're home! Me and mommy miss you. We made you something in the house. Come on let's go see it! Oh, and mommy is having a baby. I stopped in my tracks just to get my thoughts together.

Shay dropped her head as the tears rolled down her face. "I wanted to call and tell you, but I wanted it to be a surprise. We both see how that worked out."

"How far along are you?"

"I will be seven weeks tomorrow. So, now will you come home, Monta? I need you. I don't get any sleep. All I do is sit up and cry all night, missing you. I don't even leave the house, because every time I pass a Swift truck, I think it's you. When I realize it's not, I just break down and cry."

"Baby, I don't have long. Six months is all I need, and then I will be home; I promise you. Now, let's go shopping and get you guys something to eat."

We hit the malls and stopped at Cheddars and ate while enjoying the evening as a family. Then, we headed to the movies. Watching them smile and have fun was all that mattered to me. The bond me and Shay had was all I ever wanted from Miya, but that would never happen. I could lay next to Shay and hold her all night, and she would never push me away. I could walk in the kitchen and grab her ass anytime I wanted to, and it wouldn't be a problem. All I ever wanted in my relationship was to enjoy each other and have fun, but with Miya I couldn't do any of that. Shay provided me with all I lacked at home.

After the movie ended, we drove back home. I put them to bed, made sure everything was locked up, and headed back to West Point. I hated to leave, but I had to go. When I closed my eyes that night, I could see the smile that I saw the day Precious told me she loved me.

The next morning, the thought of leaving was laying on me heavy, but I had to go. I went to my truck and asked for my load to Jersey. As my load came back, I had to pick up in South Carolina. I needed an empty trailer, so I headed to Wal-Mart DC, grabbed a trailer, and headed out.

On my way, I called Sherry and let her know I was coming, and the day I was arriving. I hooked my load and headed to Amazon. The trip was great. I saw a lot and learned a lot, but the journey was over. As I crossed over into Jersey, Sherry told me what truck stop she would meet me at, and I put it in my GPS. In no time, I was pulling into one of my favorite truck stops.

I parked my truck, went inside and showered. I was walking out the door when Sherry called and said she was out front. I walked up to her, and that beautiful smile had me all over again. The scent of her long, silky hair as I wrapped my arms around her made my knees weak, but I just couldn't let her see them buckle.

We headed back to my truck, watched movies, and listened to slow jams. As Keith Sweat set the mood, she let her hair down and sat in my lap. Her kisses fell upon my lips, touching me so softly and gently as I kissed her back, picking her up and carrying her to the bed. Making the mood more intense, I turned the lights down low, and we created a masterpiece in the walls of my big rig.

The deeper the passion went, the more she fought. The kisses were something she never experienced, and the dick was more than she could handle. As my strokes became stronger, the force of the motion played the sweetest melody ever. After making her climax multiple times, we reached the point of explosion. The way her body shook from the releasing of her emotions was mind-blowing. We talked as she laid in my arms holding me tight. The music took us to places we both had looked for a long time.

The next morning, I left her in the bed asleep while I went to take my load. I arrived at my drop, dropped my trailer, and grabbed me an empty one. Then, I headed in to get my paperwork before heading back to the truck stop to get a shower. Me and Sherry traveled the city that day, enjoying the time we had together. Time rolled away from us, so we had to head back to my truck.

The tears began to fall from her eyes.

"What's wrong, baby?"

"You are leaving me, and I don't know when I will see you again."

"Baby, I promise you that I will be back," I said and kissed her then watched her drive off.

***

The next morning, I headed back down south, knowing I had to make a stop at home. As I got to Georgia, I called Kataandra to let her know I would be her way as soon as I dropped my load. I stopped in Newnan where she met me. We talked and made music and created poetry.

Over the next weeks and months, I traveled the country meeting different people, yet no one could take the place in my heart that Precious held. Every time I came home, it was always a different girl, and I still couldn't find the love and joy Precious brought.

With a month left with Swift, I met a young lady with everything I looked for but didn't know how to offer it. The week I was to turn my truck in, I got a load to Florida but didn't have enough time on my clock. I stopped in Newnan and called Shuntae.

Shuntae came to meet me, and we did things in my truck that only the walls could explain. Still, I couldn't find in her what I was looking for. It was in that moment that I decided my search was over. There was no rhyme or reason as to why my search ended with Shuntae. I guess I just got tired of the hunt, tired of the searching, tired of being unfulfilled by different women. I decided to really stop looking for things that I would never be able to find in another woman. I cleaned my truck out, dropped it off at the terminal, and came home.

Now, every day, I wonder and pray about the pain that I've been feeling for fourteen years. I don't know how to fix it.

See, when you have someone who's dear to your heart, and you know you don't want to lose them, cherish that person, love that person, spend every waking moment showing them that you will work every day like the first day to keep them. I couldn't and didn't do the things I should have done for my one true love. I can talk about it now because of the pain my heart expresses. Every day, I'm left drifting this Earth wishing I'd done differently, hoping I will find true love.

My dishonesty was the reason the one that was for me got away. Instead of just telling her about my situation with Shevonne and me getting a divorce, I made the decision for Precious. My mistake caused us a lot of heartache and pain. So much pain that I drove her right out of my arms and my life. Now, all I can do is sit and wonder, "Who's loving you now?"

CPSIA information can be obtained
at www.ICGtesting.com
Printed in the USA
LVHW010716181119
637665LV00021B/7600

9 781702 061872